TEACHING SPEAKING AND LISTENING

One Step at a Time

Revised Edition

Ann Locke

with Don Locke

B L O O M S B U R Y

LONDON • NEW DELHI • NEW YORK • SYDNEY

Second edition published 2013 by Bloomsbury Education
Bloomsbury Publishing plc
50 Bedford Square, London, WC1B 3DP

www.bloomsbury.com

978-1-4411-3980-1

First published 2006 by Continuum International Publishing Group 2006

1 3 5 7 9 10 8 6 4 2

Typeset by Fakenham Prepress Solutions, Fakenham, Norfolk, NR21 8NN
Printed and bound by CPI Group (UK) Ltd, Croydon, CR0 4YY

This book is produced using paper that is made from wood grown in
managed, sustainable forests. It is natural, renewable and recyclable.
The logging and manufacturing processes conform to the environmental
regulations of the country of origin.

Online resources accompany this book at:
www.bloomsbury.com/uk/teaching-speaking-and-listening-978-1-441-139801
Please type the URL into your web browser and follow the instructions to access
the resources. If you experience any problems, please contact Bloomsbury at:
companionwebsite@bloomsbury.com

For Grace Locke
2000–2013

Contents

Resource materials

About this book

This book introduces and explains the spoken language teaching programme *One Step at a Time*. This is:

- A structured programme for developing children's spoken language in the early years and primary school, through the active use of spoken language in the classroom.

- A whole-school programme for all children between the ages of three and nine, which can also be used in single classes with children at any of these ages or with older children up to and including those at secondary school.

- An all-needs programme, not a special needs programme. It provides differentiated teaching for all children in mainstream education.

Readers unfamiliar with the programme can turn to Chapter 5 for a quick guide to its background, content and method.

Chapters 1 to 4 provide the rationale behind *One Step at a Time*. They explain the importance of spoken language for children's development and progress in school and discuss the major problems that arise in teaching spoken language, including the size and complexity of the spoken language system, the challenge of replicating natural language learning in schools and classrooms, and the need for a teaching programme to be manageable in classroom settings. These chapters can be read independently of the *One Step* programme. They are intended for readers who want to know why spoken language matters and how this issue needs to be addressed.

Chapters 5 and 6 introduce the programme and discuss how it can be used in a school or early-years setting. Staff wishing to introduce *One Step at a Time* into their school or classroom should read these chapters first, as background to the programme as a whole. They can also read Chapters 1 to 3 to understand why the programme is needed and why it is as it is.

Chapters 7 to 11 give the detailed content for each of the five levels of the programme, including initial screens, skills checklists and vocabulary wordlists. They provide detailed advice on implementation, teaching methods and monitoring progress. There is a certain amount of repetition and overlap between these chapters, but there are also significant differences. Each chapter is intended to be self-sufficient: it can be read and used on its own as a guide to classroom practice. Staff using the programme will need to be thoroughly familiar with the relevant chapter, but they also need to know the background and how the level they are teaching fits into the programme as a whole. Chapter 4 gives a quick guide to this.

Chapter 12 gives advice on vocabulary work for those who wish to include it.

Online Training Pack

There is also an Online Training Pack available for use with the *One Step at a Time* teaching programme. This training pack includes discussion of the key factors that contribute to effective professional development; a description of five stages of professional development; and a series of PowerPoint presentations that can be used to provide an introductory training day, an in-service training course, and/or self–instruction.

The Training Pack can be accessed on the companion website for *Teaching Speaking and Listening* at www.bloomsbury.com/uk/teaching-speaking-and-listening-978-1-441-139801. The website also provides online versions of the resource materials listed in p.vi.

About this edition

The first edition, published in 2006 under the title *One Step at a Time*, has been thoroughly revised and rewritten with the aim of making the programme more flexible and easier to implement in single classes as well as across a school or a group of early-years settings. The main changes are:

● Chapter 1 has been revised in the light of developments since the first edition.

● Chapter 4 is an important new discussion of systematic language teaching.

● The 'Overview' chapters have been reorganised, with a new chapter on introducing *One Step at a Time* into a school or classroom.

● Each level of the programme is primarily intended for children at a specific age or school year but there is provision for starting at the previous level if children are new to the programme.

● There is more material on older (primary age) children.

● Vocabulary work is mostly treated as an optional element, to be included only when staff and children are ready for it.

● The detailed Procedures have been replaced by summary Key Points.

● The initial screens have been simplified.

● Classroom intervention is more varied at different levels in the programme.

● Progress through the checklists is now open-ended and not tied to school terms or years.

● New sections on Links to Literacy describe the connections between spoken language skills and reading and writing, and outline the contribution of other pre-literacy and literacy-support skills.

● Both Narrative Skills and Discussion Skills are now intended to run over two years each, but can still be used with benefit for a single year.

● An Online Training Pack is available for in-service training and professional development.

The overall structure and most of the detailed content remains the same as in the original edition.

In this edition we have tried to eliminate educational terminology that is specific to England and Wales such as nursery, Reception, Key Stage 1, etc., and focus instead on children's ages. We think of ages three to five as 'early years' or 'pre-school' education, and ages five onwards as 'school' or 'primary' education, but for simplicity often use 'schools' (and 'classrooms') for both early years and primary education.

We have, however, retained the convention for personal pronouns that adults are female and children are male. That is, for simplicity and clarity, so that teachers, parents and other adults are referred to as 'she', and children are referred to as 'he' throughout the book.

Acknowledgements

One Step at a Time would not have been possible without the encouragement and support of a large number of people. It grew out of my experience with a piece of applied research in a Sheffield Education Action Zone and was then trialled to varying degrees in several places, but most notably in Newport, South Wales, where it has been running now for almost ten years. Above all, I have to thank the schools and staff there who made the project very much their own and did so much to shape and develop its final form.

This would not have been possible in the first place without the support, enthusiasm and sheer driving force of Dr Claire Watkins, then a senior advisor with the Newport Local Education Authority. The headteachers of the first schools to use the programme – Jyothi Mathkar, Lesley Ilott, Lorraine Grange and Brenda Bispham – were instrumental in getting the project off the ground and carrying it through its first cycle. Their staff – especially Emma Jones, Catherine Place, Suzy Watkins, Sue Newman and Jenny Summers – offered valuable advice and suggested improvements when it was most needed. I owe them all a huge debt.

I would also like to thank Margaret Booth and the schools and staff in the South East Sheffield Education Action Zone for their patience and support as I tried and tested some of my early ideas. Also, Faith Cross and Chris Quinlan who were responsible for introducing the *One Step* approach in Stoke-on-Trent as part of the Stoke Speaks Out project, a couple of years before the first edition was published. I am further indebted to Faith for her support in promoting the programme since it was first published.

My thanks must also go to Faith again, and to Sue Finn, Bridget Winn, Glinette Woods, Fiona Rutledge and especially Maggie Beech, for reading and commenting on the text and materials at various times.

But my greatest debt is to my husband, Don Locke. As with the first edition, we have written this revised edition together and, as with the first edition, we dedicate it to our children and grandchildren.

Chapter 1 Why spoken language matters

This chapter explains the importance of spoken language, and why it has to be a priority for early years and primary education.

Language and learning

What is the single most important skill that children need for school, to think and learn, understand and communicate, read and write, ask and answer questions, negotiate, reason and problem-solve, express their thoughts and feelings, establish friendships, co-operate with others, and manage their own behaviour?

The answer, in a word, is 'language'; in two words, 'spoken language'. Spoken language is the basic form of human communication and the principal method of teaching from the early years through to higher education. Most of what goes on in classrooms depends on talk. Without fluency in spoken language children will never learn much at school.

Spoken language is critical for:

● **Communication**
  Spoken language is perhaps the most basic and certainly the most common form of human communication. Some cultures may not have a written language but spoken language is universal. Children who are not fully competent in spoken language will have difficulty communicating with others. They may fail to understand or be understood, and can easily become frustrated, aggressive or depressed.

● **Teaching**
  Most teaching involves talk, especially in the early years. Usually, teachers talk and children listen, but children need to understand what is said to them, and they have to talk to us for us to tell what they have learnt.

● **Learning**
  Children also learn by talking, to us and to each other, reformulating what we have told them in their own words, or extending their learning by asking questions or suggesting further ideas of their own.

● **Literacy**
  Children need to be fluent in spoken language before they can become fluent in written language. They need to know the words they read, or else 'reading' becomes a

mechanical exercise devoid of meaning; and they need to know what to say and how to say it or 'writing' becomes the making of pointless marks on paper.

● **Thinking**

Children need language to think with. We clarify our thoughts by finding words to express them, and more complex and more sophisticated ideas also require more complex or sophisticated sentence forms using more embedded clauses, and more abstract connectives and prepositions like *unless* or *until*. Children need to understand these sentences in the classroom and in their reading, so they can use them in their writing.

● **Social and emotional development**

Talk is a social skill. Children need to be able to communicate with other people if they are to make friends, join in their activities, and learn from them. If they cannot talk easily or coherently they may be isolated or bullied. Children also need the language to explain how they are feeling or why they are behaving as they do, and to understand other people's behaviour as well as their own. If they cannot express themselves or identify their feelings, they may become frustrated, difficult, perhaps aggressive.

The likelihood is that children entering education with limited spoken language will be significantly disadvantaged in school and in later life.

But spoken language, like other skills, continues to develop as children move through school. If you put a four-year-old, a six-year-old and a ten-year-old behind a screen and get them to talk to each other or answer questions, you will have no difficulty in telling which is which. The difference is striking, though so familiar that normally we hardly notice it. But children of the same age can also be years apart in their language development, and the difference between an average ten-year-old and one with seriously delayed language development will be no less striking, with obvious implications for their other achievements. It will, for example, be just as easy to tell which one is doing better at school.

And it isn't just speaking. As they progress through school, listening becomes if anything even more important. At school, children need to be able to listen – attend, understand and remember – for longer and longer periods, to increasingly complex and sophisticated language, and be able to use that information for themselves in several different ways. They need to develop not just extended listening, but extended comprehension.

There are two main ways in which education fuels the striking improvements in children's spoken language in the school years. One is through classroom teaching. Every new topic brings new vocabulary, and as they introduce more abstract ideas, teachers also introduce more subtle uses of language, for predicting, explaining, suggesting, supposing. The other is through independent reading. Just as fluent spoken language supports reading, so reading promotes a huge increase in children's vocabulary and in their use and understanding of more complex sentences.

Children who enter school with limited spoken language, however, will have limited access to these two rich sources of further development. If they have difficulty attending, are slow to catch on or cannot easily express themselves, they will not get the full benefit of classroom language, and may simply switch off from lessons they find too difficult. They are equally unlikely to enjoy or benefit from independent reading. These will be the children who are always behind, always struggling, and as the years progress fall even further behind. Even at secondary school, many remain inarticulate, unable to express or explain themselves, unwilling or unable to communicate. One study indicated that as many as 75% of pupils entering an inner city secondary school had communication difficulties which hampered their relationships, behaviour and learning (Sage, 2005).

Children's development of spoken language needs to be made a priority, especially but not only in the early years. Traditionally, however, schools have not seen themselves as needing to teach speaking and listening. Children come to school to learn to read and write; that, in large part, is why schools exist in the first place. Spoken language, by contrast, was seen as something that children learn at home and bring to school with them. It was taken for granted that they will enter formal education already equipped with the spoken language they need.

Increasingly, however, this is not the case. It was probably never wholly true. There will always have been some children whose spoken language was inadequate even for primary school. But now there seem to be many more of them. In recent years schools have become increasingly concerned at the decline in children's speaking and listening skills, their inability to concentrate, follow instructions or respond with more than monosyllabic answers or gestures. And these problems persist, through primary school and beyond. By the turn of the century it was being suggested that language delay had become the most common childhood disability (Law, Parkinson and Tamnhe, 2000). A decade later, the Communication Champion for Children reported a 58% increase over five years in the number of school-age children identified with speech, language or communication as their primary special need (Gross, 2011), though this could partly be due to improved identification.

The reasons for this increase are complex and not fully understood. It is not just a matter of more children coming into pre-school education at an age when many are still developing basic language skills, though this is certainly the case. It is not just a matter of special needs, though there are now many more special needs children in mainstream education than previously. Nor is it a matter of children for whom English is an additional language, though there are many more of these children too, as the movement of people from one country to another continues to increase.

There have also been many cultural changes that affect children's language and communication:

● parents on mobile phones talking to their friends rather than their babies, during feeding for example
● away-facing buggies replacing face-to-face prams where the pusher can chat to the baby
● the use of dummies to keep children quiet
● unspillable beakers so children no longer need to ask for a drink

● and a widespread failure to appreciate the communication needs of young children, especially among younger and less-experienced parents: 'He don't talk to me, so I don't talk to him.'

For older children there is constant TV replacing or drowning out family talk; TVs, DVDs and computer games in children's bedrooms; and the decline in family meals around a dining table.

These factors can and do affect children from all sectors of society. It has been found that children's vocabulary and simple utterances at the age of two are very strongly associated with their performance at school entry, even when this is adjusted for social class (Roulstone et al., 2011, p29). But there also seems to be a particular problem in areas of social and economic disadvantage.

Language and disadvantage

Many developed countries are struggling with the problem of the so-called 'tail of under-achievement': a significant number of children – commonly put at around 20% – who fail to benefit from normal schooling. Despite our best endeavours and an increased focus on literacy and numeracy, many children are still leaving secondary school with poor reading, writing and number skills, ill-prepared for employment and later life. Time and again, educational initiatives raise standards in general but fail to eradicate that stubborn 20% – stubborn not because these children refuse to learn but because we do not know how to help them. After more than 20 years of determined effort to raise literacy standards, the Chief Inspector for England and Wales still reports that 'one in five children do not achieve the expected literacy levels by the end of primary school....rising to one in three pupils from disadvantaged backgrounds' (Ofsted, 2012).

The link between under-achievement and social and economic disadvantage is now widely recognised. Children from deprived areas with higher initial ability do less well at school than children from middle class backgrounds with lower initial ability. Less able children from wealthier homes overtake more able poorer children by the age of six; and the gap between them 'explodes' in the early years of secondary school (DfES, 2004). There are any number of factors that might help to explain this:

● lack of opportunity

● lack of resources

● lack of facilities

● lack of encouragement

● lack of exemplars

● lack of incentives

● peer-group pressures.

But one key factor must be limited or inadequate spoken language. In some parts of the country the majority of children entering education have inadequate language and communication for the demands of the early-years curriculum. Some are barely at the level of language development that might be expected of a two-year-old. A few do not even know their own name (Field, 2011).

Studies in a deprived area of Sheffield showed that 54% of children entering nursery at ages three to four had spoken language that was noticeably delayed for their age, and almost 10% had language that was severely delayed (Locke, Ginsborg and Peers, 2002). This was not a generalised delay – their cognitive scores were around average – but specific to spoken language. Moreover, when the same children were retested two years later, their cognitive scores had improved relative to age but their language scores, especially in expressive language, had not, and the number with language that was now severely delayed had almost tripled (Locke and Ginsborg, 2003)! After two years of compensatory pre-school education in an Education Action Zone, their cognitive abilities had indeed improved, but their language skills, relative to age, were even further behind.

The explanation may lie in a landmark study by Betty Hart and Todd Risley (1995). Detailed observation of 42 American families showed striking differences in the amount that parents talked to their one- and two-year-old children. These differences were strongly associated with socio-economic status. On average, professional parents talked to their children more than three times as much as parents on welfare; 'blue collar' parents twice as much. As a result it would have taken the welfare children another seven years to get the same exposure to parental language as the professional children had already received by the age of three. Indeed, by the age of three the professional children already had a more diverse vocabulary than the parents on welfare!

There were differences in quality as well as quantity. The professional parents used a greater variety of types of word, more multi-clause sentences, more past and future tenses, and more questions of all kinds. They also responded to their children more often, and gave them more affirmative feedback. The professional parents gave their children six times as many affirmations and half as many prohibitions; and because of the difference in the total amount of talk, while about 80% of the professional parents' feedback to their children was positive, about 80% of the welfare parents' feedback was negative. By the time the children in professional families get to school, they have had several years of being talked to more competently, listened to more carefully, and responded to more positively. It is this home language environment, rather than social or economic class as such, that seems to make the difference to children's language and subsequent educational attainment (Roulstone et al, 2011).

Early years interventions from Head Start in the USA to SureStart in England and Wales have tried to compensate for disadvantages such as these but it is hardly surprising that they have met with only limited success. In the American research it would have taken an additional 41 hours a week to give children from the welfare families the same exposure to spoken language as the blue collar children; to give them the same exposure as the professional children would have taken 102 hours. Intervention on that scale is far beyond the resources of almost any compensatory programme.

These differences persist, moreover, as children progress through childhood into adolescence, reinforced not just by their home environment but also by peer group pressure. As happened in Sheffield, older children may stay at a simpler level of language development even as their cognitive skills improve. Right through to secondary school, their spoken language remains inadequate for the changing demands of the school curriculum. These children are always behind, always under-achieving. And what happens at school may only make things worse.

Language and literacy

A common response to the problem of persistent under-achievement has been to concentrate on the core skills of literacy and numeracy, and attempt to raise standards by introducing literacy teaching at younger and younger ages: to 'ensure that all children have the chance to follow an enriching curriculum by getting them reading early' (DFE, 2010). In England and Wales, for example, it is now expected that all children will be reading by the age of six, which means first introducing reading, and even writing at as young as four years old. The reasoning is that the earlier they start to read, the more chance they have of eventually becoming fluent. This may well suit some children, but what works for the educationally privileged will not necessarily work for all children. In some other countries they do it differently, with better results. Reading and writing are not introduced until children are six or seven years old. The early years are devoted instead to the systematic teaching of spoken language and other skills that make literacy possible.

We have to walk before we can run and (some special cases aside) we have to talk and listen before we can read and write. Literacy is essentially an exercise in translation from an unfamiliar language (written signs) into a familiar one (spoken sounds) and back again. Spoken language always comes first. Many people – and some cultures – never develop writing, but spoken language comes naturally, almost inevitably. If children are not already fluent in their first language – spoken language – it will be difficult if not impossible for them to become fluent in reading and writing. It has been estimated that children with inadequate speech and language in the early years are up to six times more likely to experience reading problems in school (Boyer, 1991). 'Spoken language forms a constraint, a ceiling not only on the ability to comprehend but also on the ability to write, beyond which literacy cannot progress' (Latham, 2002).

The importance of speaking and listening, including the use of phonics, is now widely recognised. But there remains a danger in insisting on introducing reading and writing at earlier and earlier ages. Phonic discrimination is an essential but relatively discrete skill which young children can learn – and enjoy learning – and use to decode print. But there is more to reading, and especially writing, than just decoding. Children have to be able to understand what they read – not just what is written but what isn't written explicitly – and use that understanding in their independent writing. Children's general language development, not their phonic skills, underpins these higher levels of comprehension.

Many children entering early education from linguistically limited or deprived backgrounds are simply not ready for literacy. Forcing them into reading and writing at an early age is pointless and counter-productive. They will not learn to read and write with any confidence; they will learn only to be failures. Boys in particular seem likely to switch off if a task is too demanding for them. And even if they seem to acquire the mechanics of literacy they may only be storing up problems for later: they may be able to decode the words, but they will not be reading with understanding; they may be able to write words down, but they will not able to produce a coherent text; they may make the grade at the age of 11 but then be out of their depth at secondary school. And this is exactly what seems to be happening (Ofsted, 2012).

Spoken language, moreover, is not just a pre-literacy skill. It is also a literacy-support skill whose continued development supports the continuing development of literacy. More accurately, this is a two-way street: literacy promotes the further development of spoken language, and spoken language promotes the further development of literacy.

Most obviously, children's reading has a significant impact on their vocabulary, on their use and understanding of more complex sentence forms, and on their understanding and use of more abstract and more figurative language. But at the same time, children's developing use and understanding of spoken language informs their reading, and especially their writing. Remembering that understanding what you read is essentially a matter of being able to translate it into spoken language, the more sophisticated children's spoken language skills are, the better able they will be to understand more sophisticated writing. In their writing, too, they need to be able to formulate thoughts and ideas in their own words before they can easily set them down on paper. Another important lexical skill that is developed in spoken language and supports both reading and writing is word-finding, or the ability to call up the appropriate word with speed, clarity and accuracy.

Moreover, the huge increase in lexical knowledge that is fuelled by active independent reading is not just a matter of vocabulary or the number of words known. It also involves knowing words of many different types, an increased use and understanding of abstract terms, and an extended grasp of word and sentence meaning, including ambiguities, subtle stylistic differences, words being carried over from one context to another (people, as well as things, can be 'sweet', 'crooked' or 'hard'), and eventually the understanding and use of similes and metaphors in speech and writing (Nippold 1998). Here as elsewhere it is not a matter of which comes first, but of each supporting the other.

Similarly, the development of syntax or sentence structure is not simply a matter of the length or complexity of utterances or sentences, but also a matter of informational content and levels of verbal reasoning. Grasping the difference between connectives like *and* and *but*, *when* and *whenever*, *because* and *although*, between verbs like *would*, *could* and *should*, or between adverbs like *definitely*, *possibly* and *typically*, enables children to better understand what they hear as well as what they read. This helps them express and explain themselves in both their talk and their writing. The development of spoken and written forms is again a two-way street.

Giving priority to spoken language

All this is now much better understood. Since the original edition of *One Step at a Time* (2006) much greater prominence has been given to what is variously called oracy, speaking and listening, and language and communication. It is no longer fair to say that spoken language gets taken for granted. But what is still not fully recognised is how deep the problem goes, how difficult it is, and how ill-equipped schools are to deal with it.

Spoken language affects more than children's communication and their acquisition of literacy. It also affects their capacity to learn and think for themselves, their social and emotional development, their ability to plan, organise, negotiate and empathise. Spoken language is, moreover, not just something they need when they start school. It continues to develop – and needs to develop – as children move through school. Supporting this development remains as important in the later school years as it is in the early years. Spoken language needs to be moved centre-stage as the fundamental skill that children need to learn, and teachers need to teach, especially but not only in the early years. It needs to be:

● the main educational priority at ages three to five

● a joint priority, with literacy, from five onwards

● for all children.

But as things are, schools hardly know where to begin. It is agreed on all sides that speaking and listening are crucial. But how, exactly, do you set about teaching them? Where do you start? What are you supposed to do? It seems significant that Ofsted (2010) speaks of 'teaching reading, writing and spelling through systematic phonics' but, more vaguely, of 'developing speaking and listening'. Spoken language is a complex system, not fully understood, seldom included in teacher training, and difficult to teach in classroom settings because of the amount and complexity of the language that children need to develop for progress in school, and because the conditions of natural language learning are difficult to reproduce in the mainstream classroom.

For most of us, our home language is like our home computer. We all have one and we know how to use it, but we don't really understand how it works, and when it goes wrong we have little idea what to do about it. For that we need an expert. That is how it has also tended to be with teachers and spoken language. If they were aware of a problem they were expected to seek advice and guidance from an expert, from a speech and language therapist or an educational psychologist. But this is no longer the case. For a variety of reasons, inadequate spoken language has become a problem that staff are expected to deal with in the classroom, without much in the way of guidance or training, and, with the best will in the world, their intervention may be limited or inappropriate.

This is because staff are not usually trained in teaching spoken language, even as a precursor to literacy. They are not taught its importance, its crucial role not just in literacy but in all learning. They are not taught its normal development, the skills that children need when they start school, or the skills they need to develop while at school. They are not taught how to recognise children's difficulties with spoken language, or how to assess them. They are not taught how to teach speaking and listening, and such curriculum guidance as exists is vague or inadequate.

Faced with children who can hardly speak or make themselves understood, who can barely form a coherent sentence or maintain a conversation, who seem not to listen or understand, who cannot describe a simple sequence of events, much less explain or predict them, staff can be at a loss to know what to do or where to begin. What, exactly, are they supposed to teach these children? How, exactly, do they teach it? How do they assess what children have learnt? And how do they manage that – whatever it is – on top of everything else they are supposed to be doing?

Issues like these are daunting and teachers cannot be expected to learn how to address them or become experts overnight. What they need, urgently, is something that will bridge the gap between their current lack of training and expertise and the immediate needs of an increasing number of children, something that will also help them develop the expertise they need, and develop it in the best way possible, through active practice in the classroom.

This is what *One Step at a Time* aims to provide. But there are three things to consider first:

- There is a huge amount of complex language that children need to acquire if they are to perform well at school. Where do we start? How do we know what to teach, when, and in what order?

- How children manage to learn their first language is mysterious – most of them just seem to pick it up – and poorly understood. How do we reproduce this in schools, especially when home language learning seems to have been inadequate?

- The mainstream curriculum and classroom are already overloaded with other demands and initiatives. How can we fit all this in on top of everything else?

The next three chapters will address these issues – what to teach, how to teach it, and how to make it manageable – and suggest an approach that can make effective spoken language work achievable by today's staff in today's classrooms.

Chapter 2 A model for teaching spoken language

This chapter outlines the complexities of spoken language, and offers a way of understanding it for educational purposes.

An educational model

The first problem for teaching spoken language is the sheer amount and complexity of language that children have to learn. The size of the average vocabulary is astonishing, and so is the speed and the ease with which children normally acquire it. Children entering early-years education at the age of three can be expected to know at least 500 to 1,000 separate words; by the age of five they should know 3–5,000. By ten, the figure has risen to 8–10,000, and by 20, at least 20,000. According to one authority (Pinker, 1994) our spoken vocabulary can reach as many as 60,000 words; according to another (Crystal, 1986) we may understand as many as 100,000. And this is only scratching the surface. The complete Oxford English Dictionary currently has around 600,000 words, and its editors estimate that the revised edition will be twice the size, with 1.3 to 1.6 million items.

And vocabulary is just the beginning. Children also have to learn a variety of sentence forms, involving words of many different types; they have to learn to put this language to all sorts of different uses, inside and outside school; and they need to develop fluency in all these skills. It is not enough that they know the words and sentence structure, and how and when to use them. Especially when it comes to acquiring literacy, they need to be able to do all this effortlessly and spontaneously, without having to think about it.

There is, therefore, much to learn, and much of it in the school years. Most children pick it up for themselves, from conversation, from teaching, and increasingly, as they get older, from reading. But if this doesn't happen, or children enter school without the spoken language they need to get started, teachers may be at a loss to know what to do about it. There are so many things these children need to learn, and so little advice or training on how to teach it, that it is not surprising if teachers hardly know where to begin.

Faced with all this, the only option is to be selective. We need to identify certain key skills and try to ensure that all children establish them as they need them. If we select the right ones it should be like throwing a stone into a pond: the effects of the initial impact will ripple out into other aspects of children's language, learning and behaviour. But to identify those skills we need a simple picture or model of what spoken language includes and how it works. Other disciplines – linguistics, psychology, sociology – have their own distinctive ways of analysing spoken language. Education needs its own model, one that can structure and guide classroom intervention.

It might seem that this ought to be a developmental model. But language development is a complex matter and not fully understood. Children vary greatly in their developmental pattern and the rate at which they progress, especially in the early years. There is also a great deal going on at the same time: children don't learn language skills singly or in sequence, they learn bits of everything together. Schools could not easily follow the course of natural development in every child, even if we fully understood it.

From an educational point of view, moreover, these skills ought to be featured not when children might first be capable of learning them, but when they are most needed for the curriculum. For example, most children begin to develop auditory discrimination and auditory memory around the age of three, but these skills do not become critical until the age of four or five when they are needed for phonics, reading, and eventually spelling. Similarly, many children are able to recount events or retell stories as young as four, including confident handling of tenses, but these skills do not become critical until the age of five to seven when they are expected to use them in their writing.

What we need instead is an educational model, one that identifies the essential skills that children need for progress through school, in the order they need them for their learning. The curriculum normally identifies two spoken language skills: speaking and listening. This is an important distinction. Children need to be able to express themselves, to state what they know and describe their thoughts and feelings; and they need to be able to listen, attend and understand. But it is not the only distinction, nor is it the best place to start. The model shown here provides a more detailed and more structured approach to teaching spoken language.

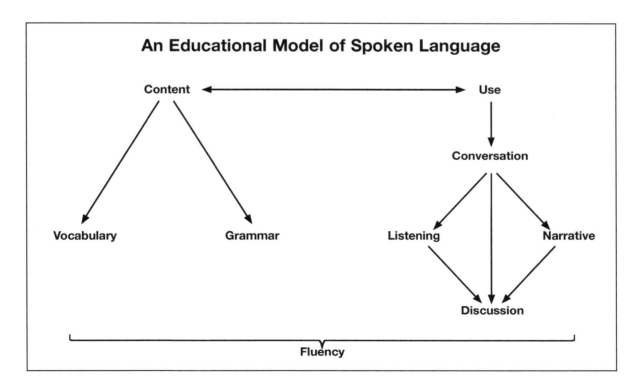

An Educational Model of Spoken Language

This educational model starts with a distinction between content and use: between the language we have and the functions it performs, between what we know and what we do with it. Learning language is like learning to drive a car. When we learn to drive we have to learn the mechanics of starting and stopping, slowing down, changing direction and changing gear. But we also have to learn how to use the car on the road: we have to learn when to slow down or speed up, how to pull out into traffic or negotiate a roundabout, and how to take account of other road-users. Normally we learn these things together: as we become more adept in the basic skills of manoeuvring the car we also become more adept in using the car on the road.

It is the same with spoken language. We have to have the vocabulary and sentence structures that give content to our language, but we also have to know how to use them to communicate with other people, in different contexts, and for different purposes. Right from the beginning, young children learn to use whatever limited content they have to engage the attention of other people and express their needs, wants and interests.

Content

The content of spoken language consists of words or vocabulary, which are the basic building blocks from which we construct our thoughts, utterances and sentences; and structure or grammar, which is the cement that binds words together and enables us to create different sentences using the same words. These typically develop together. Most children are beginning to produce two-word utterances like *big ball* and *more drink* by the time they know something like 20 to 30 different words, and more complex sentence structure develops spontaneously as they acquire a wider range of different types of word.

Basic competence in both vocabulary and sentence structure is needed before children can start on the formal curriculum, but these skills remain important as children move through education, right up to university level. Most school learning involves learning new vocabulary and more complex ideas, which need more complex sentences to express and understand them.

Vocabulary

Vocabulary is obviously essential for language and communication, and for teaching and learning, not just for literacy but across the whole curriculum. Without vocabulary we would have no language at all; we have to use words to teach; the more words that children know, the more – and the more easily – they will learn from others; and the more words they use for themselves, the better they will be able to express, reinforce and extend their learning. At school, children need an ever-widening vocabulary to understand new subjects and topics and think about them more deeply; and the vocabulary they use is a useful indicator of their understanding, their educational and cognitive development, and their likely progress at school. These points are discussed in more detail in Chapter 12.

However, we cannot realistically expect to assess the size of children's vocabulary or use that knowledge as a basis for intervention, except at the very earliest stages. As we have seen, the number of words that children need to know when they enter school runs into thousands; by the time they leave school, it will be tens of thousands. Schools cannot hope to teach or assess this number of words systematically. But four types of vocabulary are particularly important for curriculum purposes:

Early vocabulary

Children usually develop a vocabulary of several hundred words before they enter early-years education. These will be words naming the key features of their environment: the people they know, the toys and other objects they play with, the activities they take part in, the places they visit. Children with a very limited early vocabulary obviously need to develop this first, not just to understand and be understood but also to develop simple sentence forms. Early vocabulary may also need to be developed in older children with special needs or from particularly disadvantaged backgrounds.

Vocabulary of properties and relations

Children's early vocabulary consists mainly of nouns and verbs with a few simple adjectives and prepositions, but for learning in school, and to develop more complex and sophisticated sentence forms, they need a wider variety of words, including adverbs and connectives. Some children may find these words difficult because they are more abstract than they are used to, or because they can be used in different ways in different contexts (*big* difference, *big* moment, *big* idea; *on* her own, *on* purpose, *on* TV). They are also words which it is particularly easy to neglect or take for granted because they seem so obvious and familiar. Among the most important of these is the vocabulary of properties and relations (size, shape, position, movement, etc.). Children need these words for early maths and science, but they are also cross-curricular and most easily taught and learnt through practical activities like art and design, music and PE.

Vocabulary of feelings and emotion

Poor behaviour, like poor spoken language, is an increasing problem in today's schools. They may even be connected. Some unacceptable behaviour may be due to disorders or difficulties; some may be the result of poor management at home or at school; but some of it seems to be sheer inarticulate frustration. Children often lash out or resort to shouting or swearing because they lack the language to direct or control their environment, or express or explain what they are feeling. What we call emotional literacy or emotional intelligence includes the ability to understand your own emotions and communicate them appropriately, and the ability to recognise and respond appropriately to the feelings of others. This in turn requires the vocabulary to identify and discuss different feelings and emotions, both positive and negative. The continued extension of emotion vocabulary beyond the elementary 'mad, bad and sad' can make an important contribution to older children's capacity to negotiate conflict and compromise, and resolve disputes by talk rather than force.

Topic vocabulary

Every subject and topic has its key words that children need to understand and use if they are to learn it, or talk, read and write about it. Some of these words will be new: teaching a new topic is, to a considerable extent, teaching new vocabulary. Others should be familiar but it cannot be taken for granted that all children in the class will understand them, or be equally confident in using them. Topic teaching should always begin with a review of essential vocabulary, and explicit teaching of any difficult or unfamiliar terms or constructions. The older children get, the easier it is to assume that they already know the key words needed, and the more important it is to confirm that everyone in the class is familiar with them, particularly those who are making slow progress. Lack of the crucial vocabulary is likely to be one of the reasons they fall behind in the first place.

Grammar

Vocabulary is vast, grammar is complex. Grammar – meaning by that not capital letters and full stops or the right mood in a subordinate clause, but the different ways in which words can be combined together to form sentences – is a difficult technical matter requiring expert analysis. Yet, mysteriously, most adults are able to use complex grammatical constructions effortlessly and intelligibly, if not always flawlessly. Children have much to learn, mostly in the school years. The development of sentence structure is as important for their learning and educational progress as is the growth in their vocabulary. They need it for reading and writing, and for grasping and expressing increasingly complex ideas. Thinking skills, for example, depend on children's ability to understand and use more complex sentences with more embedded clauses, making much greater demand on their comprehension and memory.

As with vocabulary, the essentials are laid down early, with greater sophistication coming through the development of literacy. But while it may seem easy to identify what vocabulary children know or don't know, and what they need to learn, with grammar it is much more difficult for the non-expert to identify what children know, or need to be taught, much less know how to teach it.

It is, moreover, difficult if not impossible to teach grammatical forms directly. The most important factors in the development of sentence forms seem to be the number and range of words that children know, and exposure to model sentences at a level they can understand and respond to. Children who are still at the two-word stage when they enter early-years education may need to learn more nouns, verbs and adjectives before they begin to form simple sentences for themselves. Older children who are still using rudimentary sentences may need to learn other types of word as well, such as prepositions, adverbs, and connectives like *if*, *because* or *until*, to help them produce more complex constructions.

Two elements of grammar seem particularly important for progress in school:

Question forms

Obviously, school children need to understand questions that are put to them, but they also need to know how to ask them. An answer shows what a child does or does not know, but asking a question is a way of finding something out, of acquiring new knowledge. It also demonstrates understanding. If we don't understand something we don't even know what questions to ask, an experience many of us have had when faced with some piece of new technology. A child who asks the right question shows that he has understood. Schools give children lots of practice in answering questions but much less practice in asking them.

Questions can be of two main types: verb questions and *wh*-questions. Verb questions like 'Will it rain?' or 'Are they coming?' put the verb at the front of the sentence and require a simple yes/no answer. *Wh*-questions like 'Why is he crying?' or 'Where are you going?' add an interrogative such as *what*, *where*, *when*, *why*, *who* or *how* to the inverted sentence, and require a more detailed or extensive answer.

Children need to know how to answer both types of questions, and how and when to ask them. They need to know when and how to use different sorts of questions to find out things they want to know. If older children are not asking questions in class it may be because they are not comfortable about choosing the right question form. Teachers need to identify these children, and model and encourage their use of different questions for different purposes.

Verb forms

The most important verb forms for children's progress through school are tenses – present, past and future – and auxiliary verbs like *may* and *might*, *would*, *could* and *should*. A basic grasp of verb tenses is obviously needed for understanding time or following a story, but as children pass through school they also need to be able to understand changes of tense within a description or story, and be able to use them themselves to produce more coherent texts.

Understanding present, past and future tenses is also important not just for subjects like history but also in science, where children have to predict what *will* happen or explain what *did* happen. Similarly, modal verbs like *could*, *might* or *should* are needed to understand possibility and probability, and they are therefore important not just for science but for any activity that involves anticipation, prediction or planning. Even in the secondary years many children are not sufficiently fluent in these more subtle verb forms.

Use

Language is a tool. To get the most out of it you have to know how to use it, and the better you can use it the more you can get from it. As well as learning the words and sentence structures that make up spoken language, children have to learn how to use them to express their needs and wants, ask questions, make requests, give instructions, and for many other functions.

We have become familiar with the idea of different uses of written language: descriptions, reports, imaginative stories, factual accounts, formal applications, personal letters. It is less often noticed that talk has different uses too. We use spoken language to instruct and entertain; make friends and influence people; approve, apologise and argue. Each of these may have a different 'voice' or 'register': there are rules and customs about how to talk for different purposes, with different people, and in different contexts. Children have to learn not to talk in class the way they might talk at home, or not speak to an unfamiliar adult they way they speak to their friends. They also need to learn when and how to listen, join a discussion, end a conversation, ask a question or make a suggestion. Children who lack these skills can have difficulty expressing or explaining themselves, and may be ostracised or bullied, difficult in class, or hard to relate to for adults as well as other children.

Vocabulary is vast, grammar is complex, use is elusive. The uses of spoken language and the skills they involve are difficult to classify. As with vocabulary and grammar, it can be hard to know where to begin. Here too, we need to identify the key skills that children are going to need for learning in school, and especially for literacy. In our model they are listed as conversation, listening, narrative and discussion, because they are particularly important for the development of social skills, literacy, thinking skills and emotional development.

Conversation

Conversation is both the most basic form of spoken communication and an essential social skill. It is through conversation that we learn to speak in the first place. Conversation is also the means by which adults develop children's spoken language and provide them with a model of how language works. It underpins other learning and is the basis of most classroom teaching, especially but not only in the early years. Children need conversation not only to communicate with others but to learn about the world, express their thoughts and feelings, and make friendships.

These points are discussed in more detail in Chapter 8.

Listening

Listening is a crucial classroom skill. Children have to be able to attend, concentrate and remember, follow directions and instructions, and grasp and retain information. They have to be able to follow and understand stories and other narratives, and understand implicit or contextual meanings. The extended listening expected in school is more complex and demanding than the conversational listening most children are used to. They have to be able to attend and concentrate over longer periods, in larger groups and in a larger space, without being allowed to reply or respond until they are told to. Some find this extremely difficult, up to and including secondary level, but they may have learnt the overt behaviours of attending or concentrating, and be easily overlooked.

Listening is particularly important for the development of literacy. Children have to be able to discriminate the sounds in words in order to read, write and spell, and hearing and enjoying stories motivates them to read and write for themselves. It also helps them to develop the understanding of sentence structure and how stories work that they will eventually need for their own reading and writing.

These points are discussed in more detail in Chapter 9.

Narrative

Narrative is connected or extended talk, as in describing something in detail, recalling an event, re-telling a story, or talking about what you plan to do. It requires children to put thoughts and sentences together in a more systematic and structured way than in simple conversation. As they progress through school they need to develop this more formal type of talking in order to report events or activities, explain how something was made, or predict the outcomes of experiments.

Narrative develops thinking skills and is essential for formal writing. To write even a simple account children have to be able to think of something to write about, put it in the right order, mention key facts, exclude irrelevant detail, and provide a beginning and an ending. It will be difficult or impossible for them to do this in writing if they are not able to do it in talk. As children grow older it can be difficult to find time to practise narrative talk, but this remains important. Many children have little opportunity to develop these skills at home, and may not establish them at all without encouragement at school.

These points are discussed in more detail in Chapter 10.

Discussion

Discussion is a form of extended conversation, where children talk together about what they have learnt, how to find something out, how to plan an activity, or how to solve a problem. It requires both extended listening and extended speaking; it develops children's confidence, social skills and thinking skills; and it encourages co-operation and active learning, with children working together to find things out for themselves. Discussion can also be used to negotiate and resolve problems and differences, and develop social understanding and emotional literacy. As well as being an important life and employment skill, it is a powerful teaching and learning tool that becomes increasingly useful as children progress through primary and secondary school.

These points are discussed in more detail in Chapter 11.

Fluency

All this takes time. Even when children grow up in ideal conditions it takes several years to establish basic vocabulary, basic grammar and basic competence in language use, and these skills continue to develop and consolidate through the primary years and into secondary school. But children also need to develop fluency in all of these skills. We can again compare acquiring spoken language with learning to drive a car. It is not enough that we know how to brake or change gear, turn a corner or overtake. To be a competent driver who can safely be let out on the road, we have to be able to do these things effortlessly and spontaneously, without needing to think about them, so we can concentrate instead on where we are going, what the other traffic is doing, or what other hazards there might be – let alone talking to a passenger or listening to the radio.

Similarly with spoken language. Children need fluency in spoken language to free up their capacity for learning and thinking as well as for reading and writing. Teachers are familiar with children at all ages, right through to secondary school, who seem to have mastered the mechanics of reading in that they can read text off the page, yet seem to make little sense of what they are reading. This is because, if they find reading at all difficult, they have to put so much effort into decoding the written marks that they have no capacity left to take in the meaning. It is only if they are already so familiar with the spoken form that they can grasp the meaning effortlessly and spontaneously, without having to think about it, that they will be able to understand at the same time as they read.

It is the same with thinking skills. If children have to concentrate on understanding the words that teachers are using, they will not, at the same time, be able to think about what is being said. If they have to work hard to find words to express themselves they will not, at the same time, be able to think about what they are talking about. At primary and secondary school, children whose language is hesitant and laboured will also be hesitant and laboured in their thinking. By becoming more fluent in one, they will become more fluent in the other. If children are to use language for thinking and learning they need to be so familiar with it, so fluent in it, that the words go in through their ears, into their minds, and out through their mouths, effortlessly, automatically, spontaneously. Fluency in a skill is as important as the skill itself.

Chapter 3 Language learning at home and at school

The previous chapter looked at the issue of what to teach. The language that children need to acquire for success at school is so vast and complex that, if they have had difficulty in acquiring it themselves, it can be hard to know where to begin, what to select, or what order to teach it in. This chapter looks at the issue of how to teach spoken language, and how we can help children acquire the sophisticated and complicated language that they need for school.

Learning spoken language

Most children acquire spoken language so quickly and easily that it almost seems spontaneous. But it is not as spontaneous as it appears. We fail to notice the huge exposure to spoken language that most children receive. Talk is part of their natural environment. They are surrounded by it, not just by talk, but by talk about them: about what they are wearing, what they are doing, where they are going, or what they want to do.

Parents talk to their children almost from birth, and sometimes even before. Right from the beginning they attempt to engage their babies in mock conversations, using language they seem to expect them to understand. And, astonishingly, the baby seems to respond to their talk, almost as soon as he is able to do anything, and his responses – every grimace, every smile, every sound, and eventually every word – are rewarded with smiles, encouragement and more talk.

Later, when the child responds first with noises, then with baby sounds, and finally with attempted words, the adult interprets what he is 'saying', giving it a meaning and supplying appropriate language: 'Oh, you want a drink, do you? Yes, you can have a drink.' And when the child starts to talk, the adult adjusts her language to the level she thinks he can understand, but amplifies or explains what he is trying to say, adding words she thinks he needs or will find useful: 'Daddy shop!' 'Yes, daddy's gone to the shop to get some milk. He'll be back soon.' And sooner or later the child says: 'Daddy shop. Back soon!'

Language learning at home

The key factors in this process seem to be:

- *Close personal interaction:* Most talk to babies and toddlers is one-to-one, adult to child. The adult gives the child her undivided attention, and takes her cue from him. She can see what he is doing, what interests or engages him, and talks about it in a way she thinks he can understand. If he responds, his response gives her something to talk about in her turn.

- *Active physical involvement:* Adult and child play together or share a familiar routine like dressing or feeding. The child is actively involved, doing real things with real objects (including toys), not sitting passively looking at pictures or listening to stories. The adult talks about what the child is doing, and what he is playing with. Physical activities with physical things give the words meaning for him.

- *Familiar things and activities:* These objects and activities are familiar to the child. He already knows what the words are about – what they mean – before he learns the words themselves. He only has to learn one thing, not two.

- *Prompting, encouragement and reward:* Children are encouraged to talk, and talk is expected of them. Parents positively demand a response even from young babies, and every response is rewarded with smiles, more encouragement and more talk. At this age, almost any response seems to be a reward in itself, for both parent and child.

- *Repetition, repetition, repetition:* All this happens again and again: the same words, the same phrases, the same routines, day after day, week after week. With babies, in particular, adults seem to feel a compulsion to say everything twice. Children don't just learn language; they over-learn it.

This process continues through childhood and into adolescence, though parents can lose some of their enthusiasm for talking constantly to their children, and children can become less interested in talking to their parents. Nevertheless, parent-child talk continues to be an important means by which children increase their vocabulary, expand their sentences, and develop different ways of using talk for different purposes and in different situations.

Language learning at school

When conditions are right and children are at the right age, language learning can be effortless, natural and apparently automatic. But sometimes, for a variety of reasons, children do not have the full benefit of these conditions, and arrive at school with spoken language that is inadequate for their needs. It can then be difficult for them to make up this deficit, because it is hard to imagine a worse environment for learning spoken language than the traditional mainstream classroom.

- *Close personal interaction:* Teachers spend a lot of time talking to children – instructing, questioning, explaining – but that is not the same as talking with them. They cannot possibly give every child their undivided personal attention. There are not enough people in the room, not enough time in the day, too much pressure to do too many other things. It has been calculated that a primary school child gets, on average, only two minutes a day personal interaction with their teacher.

- *Active physical involvement:* Talk does not always relate to children's current activity, and if it does it may only be to tell them to stop doing it. Classroom activities are usually imposed on the child, driven by the daily timetable and the demands of the curriculum, not the child's interests. Much of the time they are sitting passively listening. Boys, in particular, can find this very difficult.

- *Familiar things and activities:* Schools are continually providing children with new experiences. At first there are the unfamiliar surroundings and activities, with unfamiliar adults and children. But even after that, the very purpose of school is to introduce them to new ideas, new activities, new materials. They are constantly being expected to learn new language at the same time as they are learning new things, making the task doubly difficult.

- *Prompting, encouragement and reward:* Most classroom talk is teacher talk. Teachers talk and children listen; they ask questions or give instructions and children respond. Spontaneous talk is not encouraged, it may even be positively discouraged ('Sit quietly now and listen'), no matter how interesting or urgent the content may be to the child. If children want to talk they are expected to raise their hand and wait until asked. Personal feedback is limited, sometimes negative, often non-existent.

- *Repetition, repetition, repetition:* Constant repetition and time for over-learning are luxuries most schools can't afford. There is too much pressure to move everyone on as quickly as possible. Some children never get sufficient time to consolidate new skills or develop fluency, and those who are already behind fall further behind as the class moves relentlessly on.

Much of this is changing. Most teachers are well aware of the role of active learning, of the need to arouse children's interest and involvement, of the importance of praise and positive reward. But so far as spoken language goes, the revolution is incomplete. There also needs to be a change of focus, from teachers' talk to children talking, from talk by the teacher to talk by the child.

Creating a language-learning environment

The conditions of natural language-learning are difficult to recreate in school. Schools need to reproduce them where they can and compensate for them where they cannot. They can do the first by creating a language-learning environment; they can do the second through the systematic teaching of spoken language.

A language-learning environment is one where children's talk – including their spontaneous talk – is valued, not just allowed but actively encouraged. Spoken language is a skill and, like other skills, the only way to learn it is to practise it. Children learn to talk by talking. But commonly at school, even quite young children are expected to attend to the teacher, then work silently on their own, and this expectation only increases as they grow older. They should instead be expected to be talking, to the teacher and to each other, about what they are doing and what they are learning. The classroom layout should allow children to react and talk easily to one another, as well as to the teacher.

A language-learning environment is also a secure environment, where children feel confident and comfortable, willing and able to express themselves freely in whatever way they can. Children with limited spoken language can easily feel foolish – or be made to feel foolish – if they are awkward or hesitant when faced with a task that others take for granted, but which is difficult for them. They may even seize up completely if any pressure is put on them. All children need to be encouraged to articulate what they know, what they don't understand, and what they need to find out. They need to be able to make comments and ask questions without worrying that they are going wrong or expressing themselves poorly.

Of course, children cannot be allowed to talk all the time. There may have to be rules about when they can talk or where they can talk; there may need to be designated 'talk-times' or 'talk-spaces'. In general and wherever possible, spontaneous talk should be encouraged not discouraged. A quiet classroom is not a good classroom. The buzz of a busy – not a noisy – classroom is the sign of a classroom where talk is valued.

One way to achieve this is through a more interactive, more conversational style of teaching. Most classroom talk is still directed and controlled by the teacher; most teaching is still question-and-answer, listen-then-do, initiate-respond-evaluate. In conversational teaching, staff prompt rather than probe. They ask open questions, respond to children as often as the children respond to them, and answer questions as often as they ask them. Children contribute freely rather than waiting to be asked; they are allowed to express themselves in their own words and in their own time. Teaching becomes less of a lesson, more of a dialogue.

Children's talk also needs to be recognised, much more than it is, as a way of learning. Children can learn as much from talking about something as they can from listening, reading or writing. Like adults, they will learn more and more quickly if they are in control of their own learning, and putting things in their own words clarifies and consolidates knowledge as well as demonstrating it. They especially need to be able to do this in their talk before being expected to do it in their writing.

Techniques to try

Teachers can encourage all this through interactive techniques like classroom discussion or 'Do and Review' and 'Plan, Do and Review' (see Chapters 7 and 8 of the Activities Handbook in *Teaching Talking*, Locke and Beech, 2005). For example, they can introduce each new topic by discussing with the class what they know already, what they need to learn, and how they are going to learn it. This not only shares existing knowledge across the class and helps the teacher focus teaching where it is most needed; it also helps the children themselves recognise what they know and what they still need to find out. At the end of a lesson, similarly, time can be allowed for children to discuss together and with their teacher, what they have been learning and what they have been able to find out.

Children can also learn from talking to each other. Classroom work is often seen as an individual, even solitary exercise where quite young children are often expected to work on their own much of the time. Helping one another, let alone copying, is seen as inappropriate, unfair, even as cheating. Yet children can always learn as much from other children – perhaps not always what we want them to learn – as they do from adults. Imitation, copying, and following the example of others are powerful learning mechanisms. By talking together, working together, and following one another's lead, they can also learn together.

Younger children can be given a talking partner, so they are able to consolidate and reinforce learning by talking it over together (see Chapter 10); older children can learn by discussing a topic with a group of other children, with or without adult supervision (see Chapter 11). Independent partner and discussion work give children more time than schools can normally afford for practising skills and developing fluency, while also freeing up time for staff to work individually with the children who need it. There may be concern that, left to themselves, children will go off task and become disruptive. But for most children this is unlikely, provided the task is interesting, familiar and at the appropriate level.

However the best opportunities for spontaneous talk, and for close personal interaction, occur outside of formal lessons. There are many spare moments in the day when staff can engage easily with children individually. The daily routines of entering and leaving the classroom, waiting in line, preparation and tidying up, snack and meal times, all provide good opportunities for children's talk, with adults and with other children. Children sometimes think they are supposed to keep quiet during these times; staff may need to make it clear that talk is not just allowed but encouraged, not just with adults but with each other.

All children, especially younger children, should have at least one personal conversation with an adult every day. It should be part of everyone's job description – not just teachers and classroom assistants but lunchtime supervisers, playground assistants and site staff – that they talk with children (not to them or at them but with them) whenever and wherever possible. It should be part of every school activity – daily routines, lessons, outings and visits – that adults talk with children about them, individually and together, before it has begun, while it is happening, and when it is finished. And not just staff: parents, grandparents and visitors (especially inspectors) too.

Reproducing natural language learning

With all this in place schools should be better able to reproduce the conditions of natural language learning:

- *Close personal interaction:* Schools may not be able to match the quantity and quality of normal parent-child interaction but they can still maximise the opportunities for individual conversation, making the most of those that are available, creating new ones wherever possible, and involving all available adults. A more conversational style of teaching will also allow them to respond to children's talk at their own level and extend and expand what they are saying, exactly as happens in parent-child conversation.

- *Active physical involvement:* Children are better able to learn and use new language if they are involved in activity that brings it to life, rather than just listening to someone talking. Schools provide many opportunities with the daily routines of eating and drinking, washing and toileting, dressing and undressing all providing good opportunities for teaching language to young children. Simple activities like cutting out and pasting will support language learning more than talk by itself. More practical subjects like science and technology, art and design, music, and PE and games, or active involvement through visits, role-play, model-making, or audio-visual and computer materials can be used to teach language skills to older children.

- *Familiar things and activities:* The more familiar the activity, the easier it is for children to learn and use the relevant language. Schools may be in the business of introducing new ideas and experiences but most of what goes on in the classroom is very familiar to everyone. Staff need to look to these activities for teaching language skills, so children are not being expected to learn several things at once. Daily routines and activities, rather than special or separate lessons, provide much the best opportunities for language work.

- *Prompting, encouragement and reward:* Children should be encouraged to talk, whenever and wherever possible. They should be encouraged to say what they want to say, about what interests them, when it interests them. They should be made to feel that their talk is valued and listened to, that if they want to say something it will be supported, not silenced. Spontaneous contributions should be welcomed when they are relevant, and not dismissed or criticised if they are not.

- *Repetition, repetition, repetition:* Schools need to ensure over-learning so children can consolidate, generalise and develop fluency. This takes patience, even courage in today's climate, where the pressure is to move everyone on as quickly as possible. But it needs to be done, especially with slower learners, or they will fall even further behind.

Teaching spoken language

All this will help, but it will not be enough on its own. The conditions that promote natural language learning are only part of the story. Children are not simply surrounded by spoken language, immersed in it like a baby in bathwater. Parents actually teach their children how to talk, and how to listen, without quite realising they are doing it. And if they can do it at home, we can also do it, more explicitly and more systematically, at school. There is one crucial difference between home learning and school teaching: language learning at home is spontaneous, informal and child-led; language teaching at school can be – has to be – planned, systematic and teacher-led.

At home, adults use every opportunity to encourage children's talk but without any very firm idea of what they are doing or what children need to learn. There is no plan or strategy that they are working to. They simply pick up on what their children are doing or saying, and follow that. But this interaction is so intensive and extensive – hour after hour, day after day, month after month, year after year – that children absorb an enormous amount, almost without our noticing it.

Schools don't work like that. Learning doesn't just happen. It has to be planned and organised. Lessons get prepared and timetabled. Objectives are set and progress is assessed. None of this would normally happen at home, but it is what happens in schools. If teaching is focused and systematic, moreover, children should be able to learn more, hour for hour, than they would normally learn from informal exposure and encouragement. What language teaching in school lacks in quantity, it can make up in quality; what it lacks in exposure and interaction, it can make up in focus and rigour, in efficiency and effectiveness.

This may be starting to seem impossibly demanding. It seems to mean more teaching, more lessons, more assessment, more training. Schools have limited time, staff and other resources. They are already overburdened with other initiatives, the timetable is already overcrowded. And on top of all that, they have not traditionally been expected to teach spoken language. Their staff typically lack the necessary training or expertise, and such curriculum guidance as exists is often inadequate.

But it need not be as demanding as it seems. Schools and staff need something that can take the difficulty and uncertainty out of language teaching, something that will:

● guide them in what to teach, when to teach it, how to teach it, and how to assess children's development and progress

● embody the expertise that teachers need to teach spoken language

● and enable them to develop that expertise for themselves through active experience in the classroom

but above all:

● be easy to implement and manage in the mainstream classroom.

First, however, we need to look more closely at the requirements of systematic language teaching.

Chapter 4 Systematic language teaching

Systematic teaching, of any sort, needs to include:

● **a curriculum structure or framework**

● **initial assessment of children's development**

● **differentiated intervention**

● **learning objectives**

● **incremental teaching**

● **lesson planning**

● **teaching methods**

● **assessment of children's progress**

● **consolidation of learning.**

This chapter describes how we can provide these things in the context of language teaching.

Curriculum framework

Systematic teaching needs a curriculum framework that will guide staff in what to teach and when to teach it (at what ages, and in what order). The educational model in Chapter 2 identified three main aspects of spoken language: content (vocabulary and grammar), use and fluency. They are all equally important, but use is the most effective way of approaching them. Vocabulary is vast, far too extensive to be taught systematically in any detail; grammar or sentence structure is complex, difficult to assess, and probably impossible to teach directly; and fluency is a matter of consolidating and generalising existing skills. It is through the use of language that children can develop them all: vocabulary, grammar and fluency.

The model identifies four key educational uses of spoken language – conversation, listening, narrative and discussion – which are important for the development not just of spoken language but literacy and other skills:

● Conversation is crucial for communication and social development, it is used for teaching and learning, and underpins most other language skills.

- Listening is crucial for learning, understanding, and the development of reading.

- Narrative or extended talk is crucial for coherent thought and expression, and for the development of writing.

- Discussion is crucial for the development of thinking skills, social understanding and emotional literacy.

These uses of language combine and overlap, and become relevant at different times and for different purposes. They develop together, but it is best not to try to teach them together. Instead we should separate them and teach them in the order that is relevant to the curriculum.

- Conversation comes first because it is basic to the other uses, and indeed to all teaching and learning.

- Listening skills also need to be developed in the early years, especially in preparation for reading.

- Narrative comes next as a form of extended talking, and all three feed into Discussion, which is a form of extended conversation.

- Conversation and Listening are obviously highly relevant for early years and pre-school education.

- Narrative and Discussion are more appropriate in the primary years.

Initial assessment

Assessment has something of a mixed reputation. It has come to be seen as a way of judging children, teachers and schools. But there is a difference between assessment of learning and assessment for learning. Assessment of learning is evaluation at a specific point in time: What have these children learnt? How much do they know? Assessment for learning is ongoing assessment at the point of teaching: where have these children got to in their learning?

'Assessment for learning is the process of seeking and interpreting evidence for use by learners and their teachers to decide where the learners are in their learning, where they need to go and how best to get there.' (Assessment Reform Group, 2002, quoted in Ofsted 2010)

Spoken language, however, is largely unfamiliar territory. Teachers need to learn what to look for and how to look for it. More specifically, they need to learn how to listen and what to listen for. It is not just children who need to develop both speaking and listening; teachers need both skills too. But what they need to develop is a different way of listening: they need to learn to listen to the manner not the meaning, the competence not the content, the medium not the message. This can be more difficult than it seems.

Normally, when we are teaching or talking with school children we listen to the content of what they are saying and respond to that. If we are teaching spoken language, however, we need to concentrate less on what they say and more on how they say it. How fluent are they? Do they make themselves clear? Do they have an adequate range of vocabulary – not just different words but different types of word? Are their responses appropriate? Do they really understand what we are saying, or do they just respond as they have learnt to or copy other children? Can they correct mistakes? Can they explain what they mean? Or what other children mean?

Teachers also need to be aware of differences in these skills between children so they can provide the targeted support that may be needed. Children's general ability, even their linguistic ability, is not always a good guide to more specific skills, and difficulties or delays that are not recognised at this stage can cause other problems further down the line, particularly with literacy. It is, for example, easy to overestimate more talkative children and underestimate less talkative ones: children who can chat easily enough in informal conversation may be much less comfortable when it comes to talking about a picture or retelling a story. It is also easy to overestimate children's understanding. They may be able to do something when asked – get their coats, for example – especially if everyone else is doing it. But this need not mean that they have actually understood, and the difficulties that some children are experiencing may not become apparent until much later on, when it really begins to matter.

In short, teaching staff need to be able to 'tune-in' to children's speaking and listening. This is the perhaps the most important skill they need to develop themselves. One way to do this is by using simple assessment tools that identify the specific skills that children need to develop and teachers need to listen for. These, too, have something of a mixed reputation. Ticking boxes can seem a simple, summary judgment – this child has it, that one hasn't – that cannot do justice to the subtleties of the particular case. But it also requires the teacher to attend to the particular skill and the particular child.

This is needed, first of all, to ensure that all children do in fact acquire the relevant skills. In a busy classroom some children can escape notice and it is easy to take learning for granted. But by focusing attention on particular skills in particular children, assessment tools also help teachers to 'tune-in' to children's speaking and listening, and to the considerable variations in development that can exist between children in the same class. One teacher using *One Step at a Time* remarked that she had not noticed before how, when she got them to talk about the pictures in a story book, some of her children were simply labelling things, using nouns and verbs, while others were describing them, using adjectives and adverbs. That is precisely the sort of listening skill that teaching staff themselves need to develop.

Differentiated intervention

The primary purpose of initial assessment, however, is to ensure differentiated intervention, enabling staff to provide for the differing needs of different children. It needs to identify, if only roughly and provisionally children who seem likely to:

● need a lot of support,

- need some support
- not need much support at all.

Intervention can be based on this initial assessment but the groupings should also be flexible, and adjusted when children develop and learn at different rates.

Learning objectives

Explicit objectives ensure that staff focus on specific items for teaching. If objectives are too global, they will be trying to teach too much at once; intervention will become unfocused and learning difficult to assess. Specific objectives make it clear what staff need to teach, what children need to learn, and what behaviours they need to demonstrate to show that they have learnt it. They also make it easier to monitor individual learning and ensure that the relevant skills are being learnt by all children, not just by some. And by making the structure of skills more explicit, they help teaching staff to become more aware of the nature of these skills, how they develop differently in different children, and the impact that this can have on their other learning.

To provide precise objectives for teaching spoken language we can take the four key uses of language and break them down into component skills and sub-skills. Conversation and listening, for example, are not single skills. They consist of separate skills such as knowing how to initiate a conversation or being able to discriminate letter sounds. Each of these divides in turn into identifiable behaviours or sub-skills such as greeting someone, listening to what they say, or being able to identify the initial sounds of words. With other complex skills like literacy or numeracy we are familiar with the idea that we need to break them down into elements and teach them one by one over a period of weeks, months or even years. It is the same with spoken language.

Incremental teaching

Incremental teaching is teaching that builds new learning onto existing learning in small, incremental steps. If the gap between skills is too large, children will find learning difficult. If the steps are small enough, children who are consolidating or generalising one behaviour will usually be beginning to demonstrate another one, and this provides an easy, natural transition from one item to the next, for both teaching and learning.

Accordingly, the component sub-skills that provide distinct teaching objectives should constitute small incremental steps within a broader skill, and the skills and sub-skills should be given in rough developmental order as a guide to intervention. This will allow teaching to build skill upon skill, week after week, term after term. It is also how *One Step at a Time* gets its name.

Lesson planning

By guiding staff in what to teach and in what order, this step-by-step approach will also enable them to plan lessons in advance, prepare suitable activities and materials, advise support staff and inform parents. But this need not mean fitting yet more lessons into an already overcrowded timetable. It should only mean making more systematic, more focused use of the opportunities that already exist. Spoken language is essentially a cross-curricular skill; indeed it is the essential cross-curricular skill. It is needed for every subject and can be taught with every subject. Each new topic brings new vocabulary and as subjects become more general, more abstract or more theoretical, children get introduced to more complex sentence forms and new uses of language. The fact is, teachers can hardly avoid teaching spoken language. They only need to be doing it more explicitly and more systematically.

Language work is, therefore, easily integrated into the rest of the curriculum: language work can be used to teach curriculum topics, and curriculum topics can be used to teach language skills. It should not usually be necessary to plan separate lessons or activities or prepare special materials. The class teacher may need to identify specific skills for targeted teaching, but the activities and materials needed to teach them should mostly be available already, in the existing timetable and the current classroom.

Teaching method

Teaching staff need to know what to teach and when, but they also need to know how to teach it. With spoken language this can seem particularly daunting. But spoken language can be taught if we know what we are doing. For insight we need to return to the ways in which language normally gets learnt at home, naturally, effortlessly and apparently spontaneously. As Chapter 3 explained, children are not simply surrounded by spoken language, immersed in it like a baby in bathwater. Parents actually teach their children how to talk, and how to listen, without quite realising they are doing it. They do this by:

● Modelling: providing an example, at the right level, for the child to copy.

● Highlighting: emphasising or repeating the words or expressions that they want him to understand and eventually use.

● Prompting: encouraging him to respond, urging him on with nods, smiles, comments and questions.

● Rewarding: greeting every response with smiles, more encouragement, and more talk.

This is also how we can teach spoken language in schools. Parents use these techniques naturally, almost without noticing they are doing it. Schools can use them more efficiently and more effectively, by using them explicitly and systematically:

● Modelling: the teacher illustrates the skill she wants children to learn and encourages them to copy her example. Imitation is a powerful means of teaching and learning.

● Highlighting: the teacher draws attention to the relevant skill, emphasising its importance or explaining how, when or why we need it.

- Prompting: the teacher encourages the child to respond, directing him towards the appropriate behaviour.
- Rewarding: the teacher rewards appropriate responses with praise and further encouragement.

Note that in schools, highlighting is not just incidental, a matter of emphasis or repetition. It is much more explicit, often involves detailed explanation and discussion, and tends to come at the beginning of a lesson as well as the end, and at various points between.

Assessment of progress

Assessment of progress is essential to effective teaching, not just to know what – or whether – children are learning, but also to know whether – and how far – current teaching is proving effective. This is, once again, assessment for learning rather than assessment of learning. The emphasis is less on what children do or do not know, and more on how they are learning, how quickly or slowly, and how well.

This has to be, first of all, continuing, ongoing assessment, not a separate exercise but an integral part of day-to-day teaching: 'monitoring children's progress' might be a better phrase. It also needs to be individual assessment. Classroom assessment is often whole-class assessment where the teacher asks a question, or sets a task to see if her class can do it. But this does not test everyone's learning. There will always be some children who escape notice, or can do it along with everyone else, but only with everyone else, and these are precisely the children who are likely to need most support.

The only way to be sure that every child in the class has acquired a specific skill is by checking each child individually. This need not be as onerous and time-consuming as it seems, provided there are precise teaching and learning objectives. When a teacher is working on a specific skill with specific children, teaching the skill and reviewing their progress are essentially the same thing. That is how assessment for learning works. But a teaching programme should also provide a quick and simple way of doing this.

Consolidation

There is more to learning than being taught. Children need to establish a skill, consolidate it, and generalise it; they need to become fluent in it so they can use it without trying or having to think about it, thus freeing up capacity for acquiring new skills; and they need to practice it to become fluent in it. But practice means repetition and repetition takes time, sometimes much more of it than we might expect. Children who are slow to establish a skill in the first place are also likely to take longer to consolidate and generalise it.

The pressure these days is to move everyone on as fast as possible, but this is often to the detriment of those who are most in need of support. The children who constitute the notorious 'tail of under-achievement' are precisely the ones most likely to suffer from pressure to have all children 'reading by six' (Ofsted, 2010). Children who have not consolidated a basic skill are likely to have much greater difficulty with more advanced skills later on, and may even lose the earlier skill altogether, when they seemed to have learnt it, because they hadn't consolidated it properly in the first place.

Children who haven't really grasped how to talk about things in complete sentences, for example, will be at a loss when asked to 'write a sentence'. They don't need to practice writing; they need to practice talking. Similarly, a child who has learnt both *What?* and *Where?* but hasn't properly consolidated the difference, may start confusing them again when faced with *When?* and *Why?*. When the Ofsted Chief Inspector was concerned that 45% of children who achieved a benchmark standard at the end of primary school failed to achieve the equivalent level at secondary school, his solution was to propose raising the primary target (Ofsted, 2012). It would be more sensible to ensure that primary children have properly consolidated the more basic skills.

It is crucial that staff allow children sufficient time to consolidate basic skills, and allow themselves sufficient time to ensure it. Teaching of these skills should be geared to the slowest, not the fastest, learners. Initial screening and differentiated teaching can help ensure that staff devote more time and attention to the children who most need it, but they also have to be careful not to move children – and especially these children – on too quickly. A teaching programme that sets end-of-term or end-of-year targets only increases these pressures. An effective teaching programme needs to ensure not that all children reach a certain standard by a certain time or a certain age, but that all children consolidate the more basic skills before being expected to develop more advanced ones. What matters is not how far they get, but how well they have learnt.

Putting it together

If we can put all that together we should have a teaching programme that will guide schools and staff in what to teach, when to teach it (at what ages, and in what order), how to teach it, and how to assess children's development and progress. To do all that it will need to embody the expertise that teachers need to teach spoken language, but it should at the same time enable them to develop that expertise for themselves through their use of the programme in the classroom. The best way to develop any skill is not to be told it or read about it, or even to observe it, but to do it yourself, initially with guidance but increasingly by yourself, learning from your own experience.

But an effective teaching programme must also be manageable in the mainstream classroom:

● easy to implement and easy to use

● adaptable to the different needs of different schools, different teachers and different children

● easy to integrate into existing classroom practices and activities and the current curriculum

- requiring a minimum of additional teaching time, lesson preparation, extra activities or special materials
- and a minimum of additional training, staffing or other resources.

This is exactly what *One Step at a Time* seeks to provide. Staff using the programme have said that it is not so very different from what they were doing already, but the explicit structure provides them with a focus and a method, and their increasing awareness of children's current development and the skills they need to learn, leads them to adjust their practice almost without noticing. As one of them remarked, 'It's all just common sense really'.

Chapter 5 A quick guide to *One Step at a Time*

This chapter summarises the previous chapters and introduces Chapters 7 to 11.

Background

One Step at a Time is:

● a structured teaching programme for developing children's spoken language in early-years settings and primary school through the active use of language in the classroom

● a whole-school programme for children between the ages of three and nine but can also be used in single classes, and with older children up to and including secondary school

● an all-needs programme, not a special needs programme, providing differentiated teaching for all children in mainstream education.

There is a pressing need for a teaching programme like this because:

● inadequate spoken language is increasingly recognised as a major problem in schools, restricting teaching and learning, and inhibiting the development of communication, social skills, literacy, thinking skills, social understanding and emotional literacy

● spoken language skills develop across childhood and need to be fostered in all children, not just those who are identified as having special educational needs or for whom English is an Additional Language.

● the demands on children's understanding and use of spoken language increase as they progress through school and children who start behind are likely to fall further behind

● the development of competent spoken language should therefore be the main educational priority for all children from three to five, and a joint priority with literacy from five onwards.

But spoken language is:

● a complex system, not fully understood

● seldom included in teacher training

● difficult to teach in classroom settings

- because of the quantity and complexity of the language that children need to know
- because the normal conditions of language learning are difficult to reproduce in a mainstream classroom.

Schools need to reproduce these conditions where they can, and compensate for them where they cannot. They can do this by:

● creating a language-learning environment
● providing systematic teaching of spoken language.

They can create a language-learning environment by:

● developing a more interactive, conversational style of teaching
● using children's talk as a way of teaching and learning
● maximising opportunities for informal conversation with individual children.

But to provide systematic teaching of spoken language, schools and staff are going to need something that will guide them in:

● what to teach
● when to teach it (at what ages, and in what order)
● how to teach it
● how to assess children's development and progress.

To do this it will need to:

● embody the expertise that teachers need to teach spoken language
● and enable them to develop that expertise for themselves through active experience in the classroom;

but it must also be:

● easy to implement and manage in the mainstream classroom.

Content

The key elements of spoken language that children need for progress through school are:

● vocabulary, especially early vocabulary, the vocabulary of properties and relations, the vocabulary of feelings and emotion, and topic vocabulary
● grammar or sentence structure, especially question forms and verb forms
● four key uses of language:
  - conversation

- listening

- narrative

- discussion

● and fluency in all of these.

One Step at a Time includes vocabulary work, mostly as an optional element, and systematic work on both question forms and verb forms, but the core of the programme are these four uses of language, because they can be used to establish vocabulary, sentence structure and fluency, and are fundamental for the development of literacy and other skills.

● Conversation is crucial for communication and social development, it is used for teaching and learning, and underpins most other language skills.

● Listening is crucial for learning, understanding, and the development of reading.

● Narrative or extended talk is crucial for coherent thought and expression, and for the development of writing.

● Discussion is crucial for the development of thinking skills, social understanding and emotional literacy.

These uses of language are developed in sequence:

● Conversation Skills for children aged three to four (or older).

● Listening Skills for children aged four to five (or older).

● Narrative Skills for children aged five to seven (or older).

● Discussion Skills for children aged seven to nine and older.

There is also a preliminary level:

● Getting Started for children who are not ready for systematic work on their conversation skills.

The content and procedure for Getting Started is slightly different from the other levels. It usually runs in parallel with Conversation Skills and is not needed for all children.

Each main level of the programme includes:

● an initial screen to assess children's current competence in the relevant skills

● three skills checklists for guiding intervention and monitoring progress

● guidance on lesson planning, classroom intervention and teaching method, with detailed notes on each checklist

● guidance on monitoring progress and moving on

● a vocabulary wordlist of 100 essential words

● discussion of the Links to Literacy.

The five levels of the programme are introduced and explained in Chapters 7 to 11. Each chapter is intended to be self-sufficient. There is a certain amount of repetition and overlap between them, but there are also significant differences.

Method

Initial screens

The initial screens help staff to:

- 'tune-in' to the relevant skills at each level of the programme
- identify children's current development of these skills
- determine the amount of support they are likely to need.

The initial screens are quick and simple measures of current development, not formal assessments. They identify children as:

- Competent: they seem to be acquiring these skills without too much difficulty and are not expected to need special attention
- Developing: they seem to be slower in acquiring these skills and are likely to need some support and attention
- Delayed: they seem to be having difficulty in acquiring these skills and are likely to need more intensive support and attention.

These groupings are flexible and likely to change in the course of a term or year.

Skills checklists

Each main level of the programme includes three checklists (two in the case of Getting Started).

- The checklists are used to focus and guide intervention and monitor individual progress
- Each checklist consists of a number of distinct behaviours or sub-skills grouped together under a few broad types of skill
- The skills and behaviours are listed in rough developmental order as a guide to intervention
- Children normally work through each checklist in sequence, a few behaviours at a time but usually only one broad skill at a time.

Classroom intervention

One Step at a Time uses a mixture of whole-class work, small-group work, partner work and informal interaction with individual children. The balance varies at different levels of the programme, but the primary intervention at each level is:

- Getting Started: informal interaction with individual children
- Conversation Skills: staff-led small-group work and informal interaction
- Listening Skills: whole-class and staff-led small-group work
- Narrative Skills: whole-class, small-group and partner work
- Discussion Skills: independent small-group discussion work.

Lesson planning

The checklists provide teaching and learning objectives for all children. Learning activities and materials are suggested in the Notes to each checklist.

Teaching method

The key teaching techniques are those that parents use to teach their children, usually without realising they are doing it:

- Highlighting: indicating, emphasising, explaining or discussing the skills or behaviours we want children to learn
- Modelling: illustrating a skill or behaviour for the child to copy
- Prompting: encouraging the child to respond appropriately
- Rewarding: reacting positively to any appropriate response.

Monitoring progress

Children or groups work through the checklists at their own pace and with varying degrees of support, normally one skill at a time and one checklist at a time.

Each child should be monitored separately. The checklists provide a quick and simple way of reviewing and recording individual progress.

Staff should also ensure that each behaviour has been properly consolidated, and return later to any items that have proved difficult, to check they have been retained.

Moving on

Classes may vary in how long they need to work on each checklist and at each level, but broadly:

- Getting Started runs in parallel with Conversation Skills and is expected to take less than a year
- Conversation Skills is expected to take a year, each checklist taking about a term
- Listening Skills is expected to last a year, each checklist taking about a term
- Narrative Skills is expected to extend across two years but will still benefit all children even if it can only be used for a single year. Each checklist is expected to take more than a term

- Discussion Skills is expected to extend across at least two years but will still benefit all children even if it can only be used for a single year. Each checklist is expected to take more than a term.

In each case it is more important that children consolidate basic skills than that they complete all the checklists.

Vocabulary work

Children's development of vocabulary is crucial for their progress through school but vocabulary work is mostly an optional element in *One Step at a Time*, for reasons given in Chapter 12. Each level of the programme includes a list of 100 essential words selected from early vocabulary, the vocabulary of property and relations and the vocabulary of feelings and emotion, and intended to be supplemented with topic vocabulary. The Starter Vocabulary of 100 early words is integral to Getting Started (see Chapter 7) and the Discussion Skills Wordlist provides a vocabulary of discussion, agreement and negotiation, and of feelings and emotion, that children will need to be using in their discussion groups (see Chapter 11). But at the other three levels, systematic vocabulary work need not be introduced until both children and staff are thoroughly familiar with skills teaching, as explained in Chapter 12.

Links to literacy

Literacy depends on a number of pre-literacy and literacy-support skills and experiences. Children who lack these skills or are slow to acquire them are at an immediate disadvantage. They will struggle with learning to read and write and are likely to fall further behind as they proceed through school. Early education needs to ensure that all children have these skills and experiences before they start formal literacy, and that they continue to develop them when they are expected to extend and develop their reading and writing.

Spoken language is not the only pre-literacy or literacy-support skill but it is the most crucial. Each main level of *One Step at a Time* includes information on how the current spoken language skills underpin literacy, together with advice on four other key skills that children ought to be developing at the same ages:

- *Awareness, understanding and use of reading:* Children will be more motivated to read, and more able to learn, if they understand the point and purpose of reading, and can see why it might be of use or interest to them.
- *Auditory and phonic skills:* Reading, writing and spelling depend to a major extent on children's ability to discriminate and re-combine the sounds that make up spoken words.
- *Visual-motor skills:* Writing is a difficult and complex physical skill which, unlike talking, does not come naturally to human beings; children's ability to write fluently for sense depends on their ability to make the appropriate marks easily and without thought.
- *Awareness, understanding and use of writing:* Children will be more motivated to write, and more able to learn, if they understand the point and purpose of writing, and can see why it might be of use or interest to them.

Chapter 6 First steps to *One Step*

This chapter explains how to get going on *One Step at a Time*: where to start and how to start.

Where to start

Politicians and policy-makers might not always appreciate it, but schools know that educational gains and improvements take several years to achieve. New programmes and procedures cannot be implemented all at once, and children may need several years of teaching and support before they demonstrate stable improvements in outcome.

Accordingly, *One Step at a Time* is meant for the longer term, in two respects. First, it is intended to support children's spoken language from the age of three to at least nine, and is designed as a continuous programme that can be carried through from early-years education into the later primary years. Second, it is intended to be introduced gradually, over a period of years, as children move through the system and as teachers become familiar with it and experienced in its procedures. It constitutes a learning process for staff as well as children, and in both cases it is important not to attempt too much too soon.

One Step at a Time is also intended to be flexible. Ideally, all children would follow the programme from the age of three or four through to nine or ten, but in practice they are more likely to enter and leave the programme at different stages and ages, and some may follow it for only a single year. This will still be a valuable experience for children and for staff.

This section describes how pre-schools, schools or individual teachers can decide where to start on the programme for their own particular purposes. Schools, staff and children are likely to vary enormously in what they need or can handle, but basically:

- Conversation Skills is for children aged three to four (or older).
- Listening Skills is for children aged four to five (or older).
- Narrative Skills is for children aged five to seven (or older).
- Discussion Skills is for children aged seven to nine, and older.

with Getting Started as an preliminary level for children who are not ready for systematic work on conversation.

This will map differently on to different education systems, where children move differently from pre-school education into primary school. In terms of the system in England and Wales,

Getting Started and Conversation Skills are aimed primarily at nurseries; Listening Skills at the Reception year; Narrative Skills at Key Stage 1; and Discussion Skills at Key Stage 2. But this needs to be interpreted flexibly, and can be adjusted as the programme becomes established and staff become familiar with it.

The starting point will depend on how old children are at the point at which they enter the programme, but their general level of attainment is also important. Many children, in some cases a majority, will come into early-years education with all the Conversation Skills firmly established, or come into primary school with all the Narrative Skills firmly established. But in other cases, many or all three to four-year-olds will be at the Getting Started level, and many children coming into primary school will still need work on their Listening Skills. The programme needs to be adjusted to children's abilities as well as their ages, and if there is any doubt, it is always best to start at a simpler level and then move back up when it is clear that the class is ready to do so.

Moreover, *One Step at a Time* is designed as a sequence, with one level building on another. But in some schools and classes most or all children will not have done the previous levels, and in some cases the programme may be being used only in a single class. If a significant number of children are new to the programme and have not done the previous level, it is recommended that the whole class does the previous level first, concentrating on the second and third checklists. For example, if a class of five to six-year-olds have not already done Listening Skills, they should do the second and/or third Listening Skills checklist first, before beginning Narrative Skills. Similarly, seven to eight-year-olds shouldn't be attempting discussion work without being familiar with partner work, so they should do at least the third Narrative Skills checklist before commencing Discussion Skills. Narrative Skills and Discussion Skills both extend across two years each, partly to allow for this.

The detailed guidance in Chapters 7 to 12 should also be interpreted flexibly. It is written as if it is meant to be followed rigidly, but that is only because that is the simplest way to explain it. It should instead be used in whatever ways best suits the school, staff and children. Some may prefer to follow the programme closely at first, and vary it as they gain in confidence and experience. It is important that staff feel comfortable and confident in what they are doing, and they will not feel that unless they can gain ownership of the programme, by adapting it to their own needs and purposes, and fitting it in with other classroom projects and activities.

To repeat: one size is not going to fit all, and schools and staff should start, stop, extend or adapt each level in the programme in whatever ways best suit themselves and the children in their classes.

How to start

One Step at a Time is designed as a cumulative programme in which each year builds on skills acquired in the previous year. So it, too, is best introduced one step at a time; it is not meant to be introduced at all five levels at once. This is partly because children in later years will not have been through the earlier steps in the programme, but also to allow schools to work themselves into the programme gradually without overstretching teaching staff or other resources.

The first year

The first year of using *One Step at a Time* should be seen as a learning period for staff as well as children. In recent years schools have often been overwhelmed by the number of new initiatives. These are usually accompanied by detailed guidance, telling them what schools are expected to provide and what children are expected to achieve. The pressure is always on producing results as quickly as possible. Less attention is given to whether staff might need start-up time or preliminary training to implement the new programme successfully. But concentrating on children's achievement is starting in the wrong place. If staff are not given time to practise and familiarise themselves with the new programme, they won't get the full value out of it; and the children won't benefit either, until staff have become skilled and confident in what they have to do. And, as any experienced member of staff will tell you, that takes time.

This is particularly the case when – as with speaking and listening – staff may not have had any appropriate initial training. They are going to need time to learn the new techniques and skills. The first year should therefore be a time for staff to familiarise themselves with the programme and its procedures, adapt it to their needs and purposes, and build up suitable teaching activities and resources. Experience shows that staff learn a great deal about children's spoken language in the first year of using the programme; and if they are learning, the children will be learning too.

In particular, staff should not feel the need to go faster than is comfortable for themselves and the children in their class or group, especially if the class has not done previous steps in the programme. Staff should also not be concerned if they do not manage to include everything in the programme in the first year. In particular, they might want to concentrate on skills teaching at first, and not introduce systematic vocabulary teaching until later, if at all (see Chapter 12).

Professional development

All staff involved in *One Step at a Time* are going to need some initial training in using the programme. Wherever possible, this should include:

● an overview of the programme as a whole

● an opportunity to observe the programme in operation

● specific training in the level of the programme they will be teaching

● opportunities to network with other staff, especially any staff working at the same level of the programme.

The Online Training Pack provides information and materials that can be used for an introductory training day, an in-service training course, and/or for self-instruction. It includes:

- discussion of the key factors that contribute to effective professional development
- a description of five stages in professional development
- a series of PowerPoint presentations that can be used in different ways for different purposes.

Where several classes, a school or several providers are using the programme, training should be programmed for all teachers and support staff, and should ideally be delivered by someone who is experienced in delivering the programme. Where teachers are working on their own they will need to use this book and the Training Pack in parallel, using one to support the other.

It is important not to take training for granted, even when the programme is well established. Obviously, all staff will need some training in the first year, but training also needs to be repeated in later years for staff who are new to the school or new to the programme, or are moving from one year class to another. Given the amount of staff movement in the typical primary school, some of it at the last moment, training will normally have to be repeated every year.

Networking

In areas where several providers are using the programme, staff have always found it helpful to share their experiences and expertise with colleagues from other places, especially those working at the same level of the programme. Where this happens, each level can have its own networking group to provide:

- opportunities for staff new to the programme to visit places where it is already operating, not just in initial training but also in the first year or two that they are using the programme themselves
- regular meetings for all staff working at the same level, for mutual advice and support, and to share ideas about planning and teaching methods, materials and activities.

These groups should meet frequently in the first year of using the programme, perhaps twice a term, and at regular intervals thereafter.

Programme management

Where a whole school or group of schools is using the programme they can appoint one member of staff to co-ordinate implementation within the school and/or between schools. She will ideally be someone with personal experience of using the programme, preferably at more than one level. The co-ordinator should be responsible for:

- familiarising herself with the whole programme and the background issues
- networking with other schools or early-years settings
- arranging induction and training, and any network meetings
- advising on classroom planning and teaching methods

- answering queries, dealing with problems, and noting issues for discussion at future training or network meetings
- informing and involving parents
- liaising with advisory support staff.

The co-ordinator will find it particularly helpful if she can visit and observe schools or classes that are already using the programme.

Involving parents

Chapter 3 explained how schools can create a language-learning environment by:

- adopting a more interactive, conversational style of teaching
- using children's talk as a way of teaching and learning
- maximising opportunities for informal conversation with children individually, making the most of those that exist, creating new ones where we can, and involving everyone.

This last crucially includes parents. No matter how much time teachers and other adults devote to individual children, it can only be a small part of the school day, and children spend much more time out of school, including holidays and weekends, than they spend in it. Any teaching programme will be that much more effective if it can be supported at home, and language work is an obvious and natural candidate. Parents and other family members can help in all sorts of ways, especially in providing the practice and repetition of new skills that all children need but teachers cannot always find time for.

Schools should explain to all parents:

- the importance of spoken language for their children's education
- what they can do at home to help develop it: by, for example, reciting nursery rhymes, singing songs with them, reading or telling stories, playing language games like 'I Spy', or simply talking to them about what they are doing while they are doing it. Many parents do not recognise the importance of this sort of interaction but are glad to provide it if it is pointed out to them
- how *One Step at a Time* works and what it is trying to achieve
- how they can help their children with specific skills at home: a school newsletter can keep parents up to date with what their children are learning month by month or term by term; home-school books can identify the specific skills they are learning week by week.

The best way to help parents get a feel for how to help their children at home is to provide opportunities for them to work with children in the classroom, under staff guidance. This is especially easy in the early years when they can help with simple classroom routines like getting activities ready, tidying away, or helping put on or take off children's outdoor clothes. If staff explain to parents how they can be interacting with children during these activities, engaging in conversation about what they are currently doing, this will help them appreciate how they can also help their own children at home.

The crucial first step, however, is to get parents interested and involved. Some will be only too happy to help, but others may have decidedly mixed feelings about their own school experience and be reluctant to come much further than the playground gate or the classroom door.

Staff can encourage these reluctant parents by:

- issuing personal invitations, followed by 'thank-you' letters
- beginning with parent-friendly activities like class outings, or activities specifically for parents like open days where they can see for themselves what goes on in the classroom, or a coffee morning where they can ask questions
- then moving on to classroom activities where it is easy for parents to get involved, such as art, craft and design, music and cookery, or assisting individual children
- choosing convenient times, not too long to begin with
- clarifying what is and what's not involved ('I won't have to read will I?') and any possible costs, for example for visits or outings
- talking to them afterwards about what they have done, what they have learnt, and how they can do it with their own children
- and, above all, making sure they enjoy it and want to come back for more!

Parental involvement tends to reduce as children move through the primary years, but schools are under increasing pressure to keep parents informed of their children's progress, and this should always include some comment on their communication skills. Feedback to parents of children who are showing difficulty with spoken language is particularly important, as help at home can make a significant difference to their progress at and engagement with school.

... and finally

The key to all this is confidence. Confidence is:

- what enables children to learn
- the first of the 'first four C's' – confidence, curiosity, concentration and communication – which eventually lead to the fifth C, conversation
- what children need to demonstrate in their learning: they need to be using a skill confidently, competently and consistently
- what staff need to have in their teaching if it is to benefit their class: they need to be confident and comfortable with what they are doing
- where *One Step at a Time* begins, with its very first checklist.

Confidence is often all that children need to get started, and increased confidence is what staff who have used the programme report: how very much more confident their children are in their talking, reading and writing, and their social skills, more willing to try, more engaged in the experiences being offered to them, and more able to learn from them. But *One Step at a Time* also builds the confidence of staff as much as children, their enjoyment in using the programme, the enthusiasm with which they report children's involvement, interest and progress. And that, ultimately, is what it is all about: confidence in using spoken language and confidence in teaching it.

Chapter 7 Getting Started

Getting Started is a preliminary programme for developing elementary language skills in children who are not ready for systematic work on their conversation skills. It is intended primarily for children aged three to four but can also be used with younger or older children. It normally runs in parallel with Conversation Skills and is expected to take less than a year, until children are ready to move on to Conversation Skills.

Children can have delayed or inadequate language for many different reasons: they may have had limited experience; they may be immature for their age; they may have had difficult or deprived early years; they may be unfamiliar with English; they may have special needs affecting their spoken language, either directly (for example, autism or specific language impairment) or indirectly (for example, hearing or visual impairments). Getting Started is appropriate in all these cases. It can also be used with the increasing numbers of children who are coming into early-years settings before the age of three. Some early-years settings may want to start all their children on Getting Started, either because they are younger or because so many of them are delayed for their age.

Children are not ready to begin Conversation Skills unless they are talking regularly to other people and beginning to join words together in simple two- or three-word sentences. Most children begin to use a few words around the age of 18 months and when they know between 20 and 50, usually around the age of two, they normally start putting them together. The next year sees a big acceleration in this process, and by the age of three most children are talking easily and extensively with people they know well.

But some children are slow in developing these skills and are not ready for work on their conversation. They may need to learn more words than other children, or more words of different types, before they start putting them together for themselves. They are also likely to need work on their pre-language skills. In particular, they need to develop the first four C's – confidence, curiosity, concentration and communication – before they will develop the fifth C: conversation.

Confidence is perhaps the most important attribute that children need when they start their early education. They need confidence to explore their environment, try new activities, and relate to unfamiliar people. It comes initially from close, secure relationships with a few familiar adults.

Curiosity and concentration are developed primarily through play. By playing with adults, on their own, and eventually with other children, children learn about the things around them, acquire and practise new physical skills, and develop simple social skills like turn-taking, which is later a key element in conversation.

Communication develops before children learn to speak. At least half of human communication is through posture and movement ('body language'), gestures, and facial expression. Babies quickly learn to look to others for information and guidance as well as comfort and reassurance, and are able to interpret moods and feelings from body language and facial expressions from a surprisingly early age. Then they begin to communicate their own needs and wants by pointing, non-verbal sounds, and early 'baby talk' which, guided and encouraged by their parents, soon starts to turn into recognisable words.

Play is crucial in all of this. It is primarily through play that children develop confidence, curiosity, and the rest. It is also how they develop language, through learning what things are and what they are called. And play itself is something that develops, from play with a parent, to solo play with objects and toys, to parallel play alongside other children, and then to co-operative play with other children.

Accordingly, Getting Started concentrates on developing three interlinked things:

● the basic qualities of confidence, curiosity, concentration and (pre-verbal) communication

● play

● early vocabulary.

It differs from other levels of the programme in several respects:

● It does not have its own initial screen; it uses the first two skills from the Conversation Skills screen instead.

● It has two skills checklists, not three, which are worked on concurrently, not successively.

● Vocabulary work, optional at other levels, is crucial to Getting Started.

● Intervention is primarily informal interaction with individual children.

● Getting Started is not designed as a full year's programme; children can move to Conversation Skills as soon as they are ready.

Children who have completed Getting Started should be much better integrated into the early-years environment. They should be more active, more engaged and more interested in their physical surroundings, more confident in interacting with other people, and more able to initiate contact with both adults and other children. They should be able to communicate non-verbally through gestures, sounds and facial expressions, and be beginning to communicate verbally, using simple combinations of words. They should be starting to play with dolls and toys, including constructional toys, on their own and with other children, and willing to join in other group activities, sharing and taking turns.

Initial screening

Getting Started does not have its own initial screen. Instead, children are identified for Getting Started by using the first two items on the Conversation Skills initial screen. Before children can begin Conversation Skills they need to be talking spontaneously to familiar adults and perhaps to other children. It does not matter if they are always the same few people, provided they are talking to them frequently, several times a day, and are initiating verbal contact as well as responding. Some of this may be in single words, but they also need to be joining at least two words together most of the time, to form simple sentences like 'more drink', 'bad dog' or 'daddy gone car'. Children's first multiple words tend to be single phrases like 'all gone' or 'up there', but for conversation they need to be joining nouns, verbs or adjectives, even if they are not yet forming proper sentences.

Children who lack these skills: that is, are not:

● talking frequently and spontaneously to adults or other children

● joining words together in most of their utterances

are not ready for systematic work on their conversation skills and need to do Getting Started first.

Staff may be surprised to discover just how many of these children there are. Getting Started and Conversation Skills typically run in parallel, with some children on each programme, but some early-years settings may prefer to begin all their children on Getting Started. In that case, initial screening is not strictly necessary, but it will still be useful for staff to 'tune-in' to these skills and identify the current level of development of each individual child. They will also need to use the two-item test later, to decide if children are ready to move on to Conversation Skills.

To assess these two skills, staff should first wait until children have settled in and become used to their new environment. This may take several weeks or even months, especially if children have just started pre-school. Young children often lack confidence or experience of working with adults and other children, and as they gain in confidence will show increased engagement with their surroundings, increased responsiveness to other people, and become more talkative.

This also allows time for staff to observe children informally and gauge some idea of their current skills. As well as noting how often children are talking spontaneously they should keep a rough record, over at least a week, of how often each child is putting words together in combinations of two or more words. It is important to check this more formally because it is easy to overestimate how often they are actually doing it.

The test can then be completed by two or more teaching staff working together, discussing each child separately. At this stage children's behaviour can be highly variable and a second opinion is always useful. A child who seems never to respond to one adult may be talking frequently to another. It is also easy to take elementary skills for granted, and if there is any doubt or disagreement about whether a particular child has one or other skill, it should not be credited. It is always better to underestimate abilities than overestimate them.

The Getting Started group may include some children with special educational needs but should not be thought of as a special needs group. Children can be delayed for all sorts of reasons, including lack of confidence, lack of experience, or lack of familiarity with the English language; and some children with special needs may have perfectly adequate conversation skills, or show uneven patterns of development. Children with special needs may need extra support but should be included in the *One Step* programme in the same way as any other child. For further guidance see Appendix 1.

Children who are very slow to speak or whose speech is very unclear or difficult to interpret may have an undiagnosed hearing problem. Again, see Appendix 1.

KEY POINTS

- Children who are not
  - talking frequently and spontaneously to adults or other children, and
  - joining words together in most of their utterances
  - should do Getting Started before doing Conversation Skills.
- To assess this, staff should:
  - wait until children have settled into their new environment
  - spend at least a week observing them informally, focusing on the two test items
  - keep a rough record of how often each child is joining words together
  - assess each child separately, working with other staff if possible.
- If there is any doubt or disagreement, the skill should not be credited.

Skills checklists

Unlike the other steps in the programme Getting Started has just two checklists which support each other and are worked on together:

- Learning through looking and listening
- Learning through play.

These checklists are used to focus and guide classroom intervention and monitor individual progress.

Each checklist consists of a number of distinct behaviours or sub-skills grouped together under a few broad types of skill. The first checklist, for example, is divided into: Confidence, Looking, Listening, and Communication. Confidence includes five behaviours: responding to smiles; making eye contact; initiating contact with a familiar adult; seeking affection or comfort; and responding to encouragement and approval. It will be convenient to refer to each group of items as a skill and the different sub-skills as behaviours.

These skills and behaviours are listed in rough developmental order as a guide to intervention, but different children will show different patterns of development so this is only a guide. Staff should also be guided by any skills or behaviours that their children are developing spontaneously.

Staff should work through the two checklists in parallel, one skill at a time but usually more than one behaviour at a time. Behaviours that go together get learnt together; in working on one, staff will usually have been introducing another; and this provides an easy transition from one behaviour to the next. Some children will show some or all of the relevant behaviours already, or be able to establish them almost immediately. Others may need to learn them slowly, one by one.

Each behaviour is, however, assessed separately. Staff need to be confident that each child has established it, and the only way to be sure of that is to work through the checklists systematically, ticking them off one by one.

KEY POINTS

- Each checklist identifies four general skills, divided into separate behaviours or sub-skills.

- Skills and behaviours are listed in rough developmental order as a guide to intervention.

- Staff normally work through the two checklists in parallel, one skill at a time, but usually more than one behaviour at a time.

- Every child and every behaviour needs to be assessed and monitored separately.

Starter vocabulary

Vocabulary work is crucial to Getting Started, to help children develop the word combinations they need before they can begin Conversation Skills. It is difficult to teach sentence forms as such, so Getting Started concentrates on teaching elementary vocabulary, including different types of word. When children know a reasonable number of words they normally start putting them together. But some children will need to learn more words than usual, or more words of different types, before they begin to combine them.

Most children know at least 100 words by the age of three, so the Starter Vocabulary (adapted from Locke, 1985) consists of 100 simple words that children often learn first, including nouns, verbs, and some adjectives and prepositions. These words are of course very simple but are easy to take for granted, and early-years staff have found it useful to have a list so they can check which ones their children are actually using. They can be varied if other words are likely to be more familiar or more appropriate: for example, *trainers* instead of *shoes*, *pants* instead of *trousers*, *water* instead of *juice*. Some variants, like *cat/ pussy*, are given already.

Classroom intervention

With Getting Started, intervention is primarily through informal interaction with individual children during daily classroom and playground activities. At this level it is common for children to have their own 'mother figure' or key worker who helps them settle in, plays with them, and is responsible for seeing them through the daily domestic routines. This should also be the person responsible for their Getting Started intervention, not just because the children will know her and be comfortable with her, but also because these interactions are the basis of daily intervention. Different children can have different key workers, but a key worker should not have a mixture of children on Getting Started and Conversation Skills because different intervention is required.

The most effective intervention will be with children individually while they are engaged in a familiar physical activity. The best opportunities are likely to come when they are playing, even if they are playing with or alongside other children. Staff can still relate to each child, one at a time. But there are many other times in the day when staff can interact with children individually. The daily routines of entering and leaving the room, putting on and taking off coats and boots, waiting in line, preparation and tidying up, washing and toileting, snack and meal times, all provide good opportunities for personal interaction.

Class and group activities can be used to reinforce and consolidate most skills and vocabulary. Practical activities like music or exercise can be used to practise behaviours like copying an adult or taking part in a group activity; circle-time can be used to practise behaviours like turn-taking or locating a sound; simple copying games like 'Follow my leader' can be used to teach most skills; free activity sessions provide good opportunities for encouraging skills and promoting all types of play; and all of these also provide opportunities for practising vocabulary. But in each case, staff need to concentrate on practising specific behaviours with specific children. For detailed advice see the Notes to each checklist.

A list of the behaviours and vocabulary currently being worked on should be displayed prominently and given to parents, so everyone can use it to guide their interaction with individual children.

- Intervention is primarily by informal interaction with individual children during normal class and playground activities.

- Each child should have one adult who is responsible for their Getting Started intervention, preferably a key worker or 'mother figure' who is responsible for their daily care needs.

- The best opportunities for intervention are when children are playing, or during daily classroom routines like entering and leaving, dressing and undressing, preparation and tidying up, washing or eating.

- A list of items currently being worked on should be displayed prominently in the classroom and given to parents, so everyone can use it to guide their interaction with individual children.

Skills teaching

The first step is to establish which skills or behaviours different children are currently exhibiting or developing. The key worker can start by selecting a skill from each checklist and observing her group of children over a week, noting for each child any behaviours that are firmly established and any that seem to be emerging or inconsistent. She can do this by, for example, putting a small dot in the tick box when a behaviour is first noticed, or using one tick for a behaviour that is emerging or inconsistent and two ticks for one that is firmly established.

She should ignore, for the moment, any behaviours that seem to be completely absent. The best place to start, always, is with emerging behaviours, and by the time they are firmly established others are likely to be emerging to take their place. So, as soon as she finds any behaviours that are inconsistent or emerging, she can start working on those behaviours with those children. She can then use the two-ticks system to gauge how long it is taking each child to consolidate a behaviour, and whether some forms of intervention are proving more effective than others.

In this way staff can identify an appropriate point of intervention for each child on each checklist. These will, of course, be different for different children, and staff may want to concentrate on the more delayed children first, to see if they can catch up with the others, so intervention can be more consistent and convenient across all children in their group. But intervention is always going to have to be differentiated to some degree, to meet the different needs of different children.

It is moreover essential that each child is considered individually, skill by skill and behaviour by behaviour. An overall judgement that a group of children is 'about here', or that a particular child is 'roughly there', is bound to leave some gaps unrecognised. Most children will be showing behaviours from different points on the checklists. The order is only roughly developmental and there is no one fixed pattern of child development. With these children especially, it is crucial not to take anything for granted.

KEY POINTS

- Staff use the checklists to establish, for each child, behaviours that are firmly established and behaviours that are emerging or inconsistent.

- When a behaviour is identified as emerging or inconsistent staff can begin working on it with those children.

- Each child must be considered individually, skill by skill, and behaviour by behaviour.

Vocabulary work

The key worker can first select four to six words from the Starter Vocabulary, starting if possible with words which some of her children are using already. This should initially be a mixture of nouns and verbs, such as four nouns and two verbs; other types of word can be added later on. She should put these words on a vocabulary checklist and check each of them with all of her children. If they all know a particular item she can replace it with another. In this way she arrives at a list of four to six words for initial teaching; these will probably be words that some children in her group know and others do not. With vocabulary work it is more convenient if she can keep her group more or less together, so she can use the same activities and materials with all children. It does not matter if some of them know some of the words already. They will still benefit from the extra practice.

Young children find it easiest to learn vocabulary when they are physically active, doing or using the things that the words describe. So nouns like *spoon* or *dinner* should be taught when the child is actually eating; verbs like *run* and *jump* during PE; adjectives like *wet* or *dirty* when the child is washing or drying his hands; and prepositions like *in* or *on* during PE, by getting children to climb into a box or onto a chair, or when putting things away. Physical activity seems particularly important in grasping spatial concepts. More abstract verbs like *give* or *want* are also best taught by referring to what a child is actually doing.

Once children are beginning to use a word, staff can use less familiar contexts or pictures as well as objects and activities, to generalise and consolidate learning. Any items being used to teach current vocabulary – objects, toys, pictures, etc. – should be easily available to children, so they can play with them whenever they want to, and staff can use those opportunities to reinforce teaching. Each child should practise some current vocabulary several times a day. A list of the words currently being worked on should be displayed prominently and given to parents, so everyone can see and refer to it, and use it to guide their interaction with individual children.

At the end of each week the key worker can use the checklist to tick off, child by child, any words that are being used spontaneously. If there is any uncertainty, that word should not be credited; it is always better to underestimate abilities than overestimate them. The key worker can then add another couple of words to the checklist alongside those that are still being learnt, and so on, week by week, up to a maximum of ten or 12 words at any one time. If some words are proving difficult and taking some children a long time to learn, they can be taken off the list for a while and returned to later on, by which time they may be more ready for it.

KEY POINTS

- Staff identify four to six words from the Starter Vocabulary to work on with the children in her group.

- This should initially be a mixture of nouns and verbs, e.g. four nouns and two verbs, with other types of word added later on.

- These words should be taught first in active contexts, and practised several times each day.

- At the end of each week staff can tick off, child by child, any words that are being used spontaneously.

- As well as continuing to work on the words that some children are still learning, they can add a couple of new words each week, up to a maximum of ten to 12 words at any one time.

Teaching method

Early vocabulary should be taught through simple conversation based around what the child is doing. Staff should listen carefully to what the child is saying and simplify their own language accordingly, while introducing appropriate new words. For example, if a child says 'Hot' or 'More', the adult might reply 'Yes, your dinner is hot' or 'Do you want some more drink?'. This helps familiarise children with new vocabulary and with simple word combinations. But children should not be pressured into putting words together themselves. That is likely to be counter-productive.

ENCOURAGING TALK IN YOUNG CHILDREN

Use the context as content

You need something to talk about. Talk arises most naturally from shared interest in a shared activity. It comes most easily when a child is engaged – but not engrossed – in something he enjoys or finds interesting, a familiar activity that is not too demanding. Practical 'hands-on' activity gives your words meaning for him, and his language will be easier to understand in context too.

Comment, reflect, expand

Relate talk to this immediate context. Show an interest in what the child is doing and comment on it: 'That looks interesting', 'What's it doing?'. Build your talk around his response, using any language he is using or seems to understand, but adding more detail or complexity: 'Yes, it's a *boat*', 'It's a *big* boat', 'It's a *picture* of a boat'. Using words the child used the previous turn also encourages turn-taking, even if he just says the same thing back to you.

Talk with, not at

Children can be conversation partners even at the single-word level. Get down to his level, literally. Listen to him, respond, and hand the conversation back. Use 'social oil' like nodding, smiling, saying 'mmm' or 'That's good' to keep the conversation going.

Be personal

Children are much more likely to talk about things that are relevant to them. Talk about what is happening now, what they are looking at, what they are doing, and relate it to your own experience: 'I like those biscuits too', 'I used to have a cat like that'.

Allow time

Don't overload: talk slowly, clearly, and not too much. Don't rush or interrupt: give him time to respond in his own way. Keep your responses at a level he can easily understand.

Take care with questions

Don't cross-examine. Avoid test questions like 'What colour is that?'. Questions should be comments like 'Isn't that good?' or clarifications like 'Why is he crying?'. Open questions like 'What shall we do next?' can be difficult for young children. Yes/no questions like 'Do you want the truck?' are easier but do not stimulate children's language. Questions that provide alternatives, like 'Do you want the truck or the car?', help them develop it.

adapted with permission from Webster (1987)

But some behaviours and vocabulary will need to be taught more explicitly. The most effective teaching techniques are those that parents use to teach their children, usually without realising they are doing it (see Chapter 3):

● Highlighting: the adult draws attention to the word or behaviour by emphasising it or pointing it out: 'Look how Johnny is marching to the music!', 'Mia is playing with Jenny. That looks fun!'

● Modelling: the adult illustrates the behaviour she wants children to learn. Imitation is a powerful means of teaching and learning but at this early stage, as well as modelling relevant behaviour themselves for the children to copy, staff are as likely to use children's behaviour as a model for their intervention. For example, if the child points at something the adult points at it too, says what it is, and talks about it. This is a particularly effective way of highlighting behaviours with young children.

● Prompting: the adult encourages the child to respond, directing him towards the appropriate behaviour: for example, 'Now you do it too', 'Can Sam play with you?'. If a response is not quite what she is looking for, she can encourage a more appropriate response by asking questions, prompting or modelling the skill again.

● Rewarding: the adult rewards any appropriate response with praise and further encouragement. Praise will be more effective if it can emphasise what was good about the response: 'That pointing was good. Now I know what you want', 'You played with that bus for such a long time', 'Thank you for letting Meera have a turn'. Indiscriminate praise – praising anything and everything that children say or do – does not help them to learn.

Suitable activities for teaching some behaviours are suggested in the Notes to each checklist.

Monitoring progress

Continuing assessment of children's progress is crucial for effective teaching, particularly with spoken language where it is so easy to overestimate children's abilities, or move them on before learning has been properly consolidated. Many – perhaps most – will already have the early behaviours in Checklist 1. But some may not, and the only way of knowing for sure which is which, and exactly which behaviours they do have, is by observing each child individually.

This need not be as onerous and time-consuming as it seems. The checklists provide a quick and simple way of recording individual progress. As each child exhibits a behaviour or uses a word confidently, competently and consistently, it is ticked off on the checklist. This should not be on the basis of a single occasion. Each behaviour needs to be consistent – repeated and reliable – as well as confident and competent. The best test is whether children are showing the behaviour or using the word spontaneously, without adult intervention. As with the initial screen, if there is any doubt or disagreement about a particular item, it should not be credited. It is always better to underestimate children's abilities than overestimate them.

Moving on

Staff should normally continue working on a particular item until a child has learnt it. Early-years staff sometimes think they need to keep changing stories or activities to retain children's interest and extend their experience, but, as every parent knows, young children like to repeat the same things over and over again: the same stories, the same songs, the same little phrases, the same little routines, day after day. Children under five will always benefit from repeating activities, particularly if they are having difficulty with the language that goes with them.

It is however also important not to get stuck on items that are proving particularly difficult. If a child shows any degree of stress, staff should leave that item for the moment, move to another one, and come back to it again later, by which time the child may be more ready for it.

Staff should continue working through the checklists item by item until each child is ready to move on to Conversation Skills. Some children may improve and move up to Conversation Skills fairly quickly; others may not. They do not need to complete both checklists, or acquire all the Starter Vocabulary. Strictly, all they need do is satisfy the initial two-part test, that they are now:

● talking frequently and spontaneously to adults or other children, and

● joining words together in most of their utterances.

Staff should review this from time to time, perhaps once a month, or once or twice a term. They should first note whether children are now talking frequently and spontaneously and then keep a rough record over about a week of how often they are actually using combinations of two or more words. It is important to check this explicitly because it is easy to overestimate how often they are actually doing it.

If children have satisfied this double test they can move to Conversation Skills. This can happen at any time, and will happen at different times for different children, but it will usually be more convenient to move them in a group, or at the end of a term, rather than one at a time. The sooner they can move on, the more progress they will be able to make on Conversation Skills. But it is also important not to do this too quickly. These children are likely to need as much practice and consolidation in basic skills as they can get. If they are still obviously lacking some essential skills or have a plainly inadequate vocabulary, it may be better to keep them on Getting Started for the time being.

When children do move to Conversation Skills they should first be assessed on the initial screen and assigned to teaching groups as described in Chapter 8. Some of these children may not be able to complete Conversation Skills by the end of the year.

KEY POINTS

- Staff normally continue working on an item until each child has learnt it, but it may sometimes be better to leave a difficult item and come back to it again later.

- They should review children once a month, or once or twice a term, to consider whether they are ready to move to Conversation Skills, i.e. whether they are now

  - talking frequently and spontaneously to adults or other children, and

  - joining words together in most of their utterances.

- They should first note whether children are talking frequently and spontaneously, and then keep a rough record over about a week of how often they are actually using combinations of two or more words.

- Children who satisfy this test can move to Conversation Skills at any time. They do not need to have completed both checklists or have learnt all the Starter Vocabulary. But it may be simpler to move children on in a group, rather than one by one.

Teaching Speaking and Listening © Ann Locke (Bloomsbury Publishing plc, 2013)

Child's name												
Confidence												
Responds to smiles, will make eye contact												
Initiates contact with familiar adults												
Will seek affection, comfort, etc. from a familiar adult												
Responds to encouragement and approval												
Looking												
Shows interest in their surroundings												
Responds appropriately to pointing												
Copies adults or other children												
Examines unfamiliar objects or toys												
Will look at pictures with an adult												
Will follow a picture book with an adult												
Listening												
Can recognise some things by their sound												
In small group, will attend to a person who is talking												
Joins in action games and songs												
Will try to march or clap in time to familiar music												
Shows understanding of nouns and verbs without visual cues												
Communication												
Shows interest in other children												
Interacts with other children												
Will join in group activities led by an adult												
Responds to facial expressions												
Communicates by pointing or facial expressions												
Communicates vocally with adults and other children												
Gives at least one-word response to questions												

Teaching Speaking and Listening © Ann Locke (Bloomsbury Publishing plc, 2013)

Child's name

Solo play												
Solitary play with materials, objects, toys etc.												
Parallel play (alongside but not with other children)												
Taking turns												
Understands simple turn-taking like passing a ball backwards and forwards												
Can wait for turn in familiar activities and routines												
Can wait for turn in unfamiliar activities												
Playing with others												
Simple informal games with adults, e.g. hiding and finding things												
Imitative play (copying adults or other children)												
Informal games with other children, e.g. chasing and hiding												
Will help other children when asked												
Will include other children in play												
Will share toys etc. with other children												
Imaginative play												
Simple play with musical instruments, craft materials, etc.												
Constructive play with sand, dough, bricks, etc.												
Creative play (simple art and craft work)												
Simple pretend play with dolls, toys, etc.												

Getting Started

Starter vocabulary

Nouns

baby	ball	apple
Daddy	bike	biscuit
man	bricks	dinner
Mummy	bus	plate
	car	spoon
eyes	doll	sweets
feet	duck	
hair	pram	cup
hands	swing	drink
mouth	Teddy/bear	milk
nose		orange/juice
toes	book	water
tummy/belly	box	
	paper	bed
bag	pencil	chair
dress		house
hat	bird	table
jacket	cat/pussy	
pants/knickers	dog	brush
shoes	flower	soap
socks	tree	tap
trousers		towel

Verbs

brush	come
clap	find
cool	get
cry	give
cut	like/love
drink	look (at)
dry	make
eat	play
hit	put
jump	want
kick	
push	
read	
run	
sit	
sleep	
stand	
throw	
walk	
wash	

Other words

big
dirty
hot
wet
down
in
on
up
gone
more
yes
no

Teaching Speaking and Listening © Ann Locke (Bloomsbury Publishing plc, 2013)

NOTES ON CHECKLIST 1

Learning through looking and listening

This checklist develops children's confidence and the basic pre-verbal skills of looking, listening and non-verbal communication.

Confidence

Confidence is perhaps the most important attribute that children need when they start their early education. It can take some children several weeks to gain the confidence they need to explore their new environment, try new activities, and relate to unfamiliar adults or other children. They will need a secure and protective environment, and a warm and trusting relationship with one or more of the staff. Staff can build children's confidence through physical contact, talking to them, showing approval and highlighting successes, and promoting friendships with other children. Giving and rewarding simple responsibilities, such as getting something or taking it to someone else, are good ways of building children's confidence.

Most children will show the behaviours in this part of the checklist once they start feeling secure with an adult or other children. Staff can promote particular responses by doing things with them, giving them things to play with, and rewarding any response with smiles and encouragement.

Looking

Children learn a great deal both from looking at their surroundings and from looking at other people, but may lack the confidence to do this in unfamiliar situations or with unfamiliar adults. They may need to be encouraged to explore and handle things for themselves, or to respond when adults point things out to them.

Children who have learnt to look to others for reassurance and guidance will begin to copy their behaviour and reactions. Copying may have to be one-to-one (teacher-child) at first, before including children in group activities like 'Follow my leader' or 'This is the way we wash our hands'. At this stage, looking at pictures or picture books may also need to be one-to-one, so the adult can be sure that the child understands or recognises what is happening.

Listening

Listening is important, not just for learning to talk but for understanding what goes on in the classroom. If children are slow to respond to speech staff need to be sure they can hear what is being said, and make appropriate arrangements if they are having any difficulty. But there is more to listening than just hearing. Children also need to be able to recognise different sounds, including the sounds of the human voice, and appreciate their significance, including the significance of talk as a means of communication.

Most children should be able to recognise familiar sounds like the classroom bell, musical toys, sirens, birds singing or dogs barking. This can be taught and tested using barrier games like 'What made that noise?'. But many children will find listening in a group more difficult than listening one-to-one. They may not even realise that the adult is talking to them, and staff may have to get their attention by naming them individually: 'Are you listening, Jason?'.

Action games and songs like 'Miss Polly had a dolly' or 'The wheels on the bus' will also help children to listen in a group. At this age many children find marching or clapping in time to music difficult. What is needed here is that they can at least try to do it – that is, that they recognise what they are supposed to do – even if they cannot accurately do it.

Understanding without visual cues involves responding appropriately to nouns and/or verbs ('Throw the ball', 'Get the bricks') without the adult pointing or demonstrating the action. This will normally be learnt as part of vocabulary work, but the adult may need to practise it frequently with the child before he is able to do it on his own.

Communication

Helping children develop non-verbal communication is crucial for the emergence of spoken language. This includes looking, smiling and other facial expressions, touches and gestures, and shared activity. Some children may need to be helped to engage with other children, and to respond to them.

Staff should look for opportunities where they can demonstrate facial expressions or simple physical gestures like pointing out things of interest, shrugging their shoulders, or clapping their hands to show they are pleased. Some children may also need to be taught non-verbal vocal communication such as clapping, or calling out to indicate something or attract someone's attention.

The simplest form of verbal communication is indicating wants and needs by naming things: *drink!*, *biscuit!*

NOTES ON CHECKLIST 2

Learning through play

This checklist develops children's play as a means of developing confidence, curiosity, concentration and communication. Play is one of the most important ways in which children learn about the world around them and about other people. It:

● teaches children how to explore the physical world

● enables them to practise the basic physical skills of handling materials, using tools, etc.

● helps them discover their abilities, and what they like and dislike doing

- teaches them how to interact with adults and get on with other children
- encourages simple communication with adults and with other children, and provides practice in talk
- gives children something to talk about and reasons to communicate, for example to get help or co-ordinate behaviour
- teaches them to listen and respond, which is crucial for conversation.

Children who seem to be just playing may actually be learning more than they will learn from any lesson, and the extent to which they talk while playing, to themselves or to others, is a good measure of their communication skills. Children who are slow in acquiring communication skills may need more play, over a longer period, than other children. Children who play silently need to be encouraged to talk about what they are doing.

Children's play takes different forms and develops through a number of stages, as shown in the chart: 'The Development of Play'. This lists typical activities that can be used in teaching or encouraging the different types of play at different developmental stages.

Staff should first take time to observe each child in their spontaneous play and get some idea of their current development and the skills they currently have or lack. Some children will move easily from one type of play to another as they gain more experience and more confidence. Others may need to be encouraged and rewarded more explicitly, with the teacher carefully introducing them to new activities or situations, and showing them how to play by playing with them.

Turn-taking is particularly important, both as a social behaviour and as preparation for the to-and-fro of conversation. Children may need to learn both how to take turns – for example, passing an object and taking it back again – and when to take a turn. Or they may have learnt how to wait their turn in familiar activities, but find it difficult to wait in an exciting new activity, such as stirring the cooking mixture or playing with a new piece of equipment. Staff may have to model and encourage these behaviours.

Play with other children should not be hurried. Children who are still at the stages of solitary or parallel play can be encouraged to watch other children playing and tolerate other children's presence during their own play, but they should not be made to play with them if they are not ready. Friendships can be encouraged by grouping children who have similar abilities and interests, and are likely to be friendly without being dominating or over-protective. Some children may also need to be encouraged to involve themselves in activities such as playing with equipment or large toys (riding, pulling, pushing, etc.), physical play (rough and tumble) or creative and pretend play.

Staff can encourage different types of play by:

- providing frequent opportunities and appropriate materials
- playing with them at their current level of development, and involving other children and adults as appropriate
- ensuring that they engage in a range of activities and don't spend all their time in just one type of play.

The development of play

Types of play	Physical play	Constructional play	Table-top play	Pretend play
Up to about two years: **Early exploration** Children explore their physical environment, developing curiosity **Solo play** Children play on their own but may like a familiar adult nearby **Parallel play** Children play alongside but not with other children	Rough and tumble play with adults Water play, e.g. paddling, splashing Play with sand Push-and-pull or sit-and-ride toys, e.g. toy cars, bikes, etc.	Play with activity centres, blocks, bricks, play dough, modelling clay, etc. Making mud pies, sand castles, dough cakes, etc. Play with stacking or nesting boxes or beakers, posting boxes, insert boards, etc.	Cutting and pasting Painting, colouring, drawing using crayons, pencils, finger paints, etc.	Play with musical objects and instruments (rattles, shakers, drums, etc.). Hiding and finding Play with household objects (brushes, saucepans, etc.) Pretend play with dolls, toys, shoes, hats, bags, cardboard boxes
About two to four years: **Imitative play** Children copy adult behaviour or the play of other children **Play with others** Children join in activities with other children, sharing, taking turns, etc. **Co-operative play** Children develop joint activities with other children	Climbing, jumping, balancing Swings and slides Kicking, throwing, catching beanbags, balls etc. Rough and tumble with other children, e.g. chasing, hiding	Building walls, towers, making models with bricks, Duplo, Lego, etc. Large-piece jigsaw puzzles	Work with scissors, crayons, paintbrushes, glue etc to produce pictures, cards, collages, friezes etc. Small-piece jigsaw puzzles	Dressing up Copying adults ('helping' to cook, sweep, fix the car, etc.) Pretend social routines (cooking, cleaning, driving a bus, going to bed, etc.) Pretend social settings (playing houses, shops, doctor/dentist, post office, etc.)
From about four years: **Imaginative play** Children use their imaginations to make things, create situations and stories, etc. **Rule-governed play** Children understand and take part in rule-governed activities	Hide and seek, Kiss chase, Statue tig, British bulldog, etc. Races, obstacle courses, team games	Making models with and without instruction; with and without guidance; and with and without other children	Free and directed art and design work with and without adult help Board and card games	Using props to act out real life situations Fantasy games with other children

Teaching Speaking and Listening © Ann Locke (Bloomsbury Publishing plc, 2013)

Chapter 8 Conversation Skills

Conversation Skills is a programme for developing children's ability to talk easily and fluently with adults and other children, as a way of developing the language skills they need for literacy and other aspects of the early school curriculum. It is intended for children aged three to four but some children of this age, and possibly older, are not ready for systematic work on their conversation skills and should do Getting Started first. Conversation Skills is expected to take about a year to complete but it is more important that children consolidate basic skills than that they finish this level of the programme.

Conversation is the most basic of all language skills. It is through conversation that we learn to speak in the first place. Parents talk to their babies almost from birth and their babies respond at an astonishingly early age, at first with interest and facial expressions, then with noises and baby sounds. These mock conversations, with parents talking to their babies and the babies 'talking' back, are the foundation of spoken language. By the age of two or three most children are enthusiastic conversationalists, eager to talk with familiar adults and sometimes difficult to stop. But children who have not had the same encouragement to talk with their parents may have restricted conversation skills even at four or five.

Conversation is also a basic social skill. It is through conversation that we learn to relate to other people, adults and children. We use conversation to make initial contact, maintain friendships, co-ordinate our actions, and resolve disagreements. Without conversation children will be isolated and limited in their ability to influence what is going on around them.

Conversation is also the basis of most learning and teaching, especially but not only in the early years. We use conversation to teach young children about the world around them, by talking with them about what they are doing or things that have attracted their attention, and we use their replies to gauge what they know and what they still need to learn.

We also use conversation to teach spoken language itself; it is a skill children need to learn in order to acquire other language skills. We teach both vocabulary and sentence structure through conversation, building on what children are saying and adding new words or more structure: 'Ball!'. 'Yes, that's a ball. Isn't it a *big* ball!'. We use conversation to assess their understanding, picking up on things that they seem not to have grasped or asking them questions. And conversation introduces children by easy stages to the idea of a sequence of sentences, and hence to the idea of an account, an explanation or a narrative.

Conversation is more than just talk. To hold a conversation children need a basic vocabulary; they need to be able to join words together to form sentences; they need to be able to describe and comment on things going on around them; they need to be able to answer questions and, every bit as importantly, be able to ask questions. But they also need a number of social linguistic skills (sometimes called 'conversational etiquette') such as knowing how to make social contact with other people; how to respond and take turns as speaker and as listener; how to follow and keep to a topic, or change it appropriately; how to start or end a conversation properly; and what to do if others haven't understood them.

Children also need to be able to use conversation in different contexts and for different purposes: commenting, directing, asking, expressing feelings, needs and wants, and agreeing or negotiating plans and actions. It is important to ensure that their conversation skills are not limited to particular topics or situations – and in particular not to small-group teaching sessions! We should not assume that because children can demonstrate a particular skill in small-group or one-to-one conversations, they will be able to use it spontaneously in other contexts.

Most children are capable of holding an extended conversation by the age of three, and by the time they are four staff and parents may be more interested in finding ways of stopping them talking. But at this age they still have much to learn about conversation, including stopping, starting and staying on topic. More sophisticated skills, like changing the topic smoothly, or adapting what they say and how they say it to different contexts and conversational partners, continue to develop up to and including secondary school.

On the other hand, many children entering early-years education have very rudimentary conversation skills, if they have any at all. They may not even have sufficient language skills for systematic work on their conversation, and will need to work through the preliminary level, Getting Started, as described in the previous chapter and the next section.

Children who have completed Conversation Skills will be much more confident, socially and linguistically. They will be willing to talk with different people about different things, in different situations and during different activities, both about what they are doing and about things that happen inside and outside school. They will understand and be able to use significantly more complex sentences. They will be able to learn about the world through talk as well as through physical contact and play, and be starting to explain and predict things as well as describe them.

Initial screening

The initial screen helps staff:

- 'tune-in' to the relevant skills at this level of the programme
- identify children's current development of these skills
- determine the amount of support they are likely to need.

The first of these may be the most important. For Conversation Skills staff need to be particularly aware of children's fluency, their ability to talk easily and readily with different people and in different situations, and their ability to use language for different purposes, especially purposes that are important in early-years education, such as naming, reporting, responding, greeting, asking and directing.

They also need to be aware of the differences in these skills between children, so they can provide the targeted support that is needed. Which children are fluent? Make themselves clear? Use different types of word? Respond appropriately to other children?

All this can be more difficult than it might seem. Staff may not be used to discriminating these behaviours, or identifying them in individual children. These are the skills they need to develop, and the screening process can help them do it.

The initial screen is a quick and simple measure of current development, not a formal assessment. It identifies children as:

● Competent: they seem to be acquiring these skills without too much difficulty and are not expected to need special attention.

● Developing: they seem to be slower in acquiring these skills and are likely to need some support and attention.

● Delayed: they seem to be having difficulty in acquiring these skills and are likely to need more intensive support and attention.

● Getting Started: children who lack the basic skills needed for conversation and need to do Getting Started first.

These groupings are intended to be flexible and are likely to change in the course of a term or year.

Before children can begin Conversation Skills they need to be talking to familiar adults and perhaps to other children. It does not matter if they are always the same few people, provided they are talking to them frequently, several times a day, and spontaneously, that is, initiating as well as responding. Some of this may be in single words, but they also need to be joining words together most of the time to form simple sentences like 'more drink', 'bad dog' or 'daddy gone car'. When children first begin to join words they tend to be little phrases like 'all gone' or 'up there', but for conversation they need to be joining nouns, verbs or adjectives, even if they are not yet forming proper sentences. Children who lack either of these skills: that is, are not:

● talking frequently and spontaneously to adults or other children, and

● joining words together in most of their utterances

are not ready for systematic work on their conversation skills, and need to do Getting Started instead. Staff may be surprised to discover just how many of these children there are. Getting Started and Conversation Skills typically run in parallel, with some children on each programme, but some early-years settings may prefer to begin all their children on Getting Started.

Screening should not be carried out until children have settled into their new class and become used to their new environment. This may take several weeks or even months, especially if children have just started pre-school. Young children often lack confidence or experience of working with adults and other children, and as they gain in confidence will show increased engagement with their surroundings, increased responsiveness to other people, and become more talkative.

This also allows time for staff to observe children informally in a variety of situations, focusing on the behaviours to be assessed. As well as noting how often children are talking spontaneously, they should keep a rough record for each child, over about a week, of how often they are putting words together in combinations of two or more words. It is important to check this more formally because it is easy to overestimate how often they are actually doing it.

The screen can then be completed, working together with a colleague. Children's behaviour can be variable at this age and a second opinion is always useful. It is also easy to take some of these behaviours for granted, or underestimate the skills of quiet children and overestimate the skills of more talkative ones.

Each child needs to be considered separately. Staff are often surprised to discover that while it seems 'the whole class' can do something, there is actually huge variation with some children barely understanding what the task is.

It is also important to consider each behaviour separately. A behaviour should only be credited if a child is using it confidently, competently and consistently. If there is any doubt or disagreement, the behaviour should not be credited. It is always better to underestimate children's abilities than overestimate them.

Unlike the other initial screens, the Conversation Skills screen has three bands because it includes a baseline test for Getting Started. All children are assessed band by band. That is, if they do not have all the behaviours in Band 1, they do not need to be assessed on Band 2; and if they do not have all the behaviours in Band 2, they do not need to be assessed on Band 3.

● Children who lack either behaviour in Band 1 should do Getting Started instead.

● Children who have both behaviours in Band 1 but lack any of the behaviours in Band 2 are identified as Delayed, even if they have some of the behaviours in Band 3.

● Children who have all the behaviours in Bands 1 and 2 but lack any of the behaviours in Band 3 are identified as Developing.

● Children who have all the behaviours in all three bands are identified as Competent.

The Delayed group may include some children with special educational needs but should not be thought of as a special needs group. Children can be Delayed for all sorts of reasons, including lack of confidence, lack of experience, or lack of familiarity with the English language; and some children with special needs may have perfectly adequate conversation skills, or show uneven patterns of development. Children with special needs may need extra support but should be included in the *One Step* programme in the same way as any other child. For further guidance see Appendix 1.

Children who are slow to speak or whose speech is very unclear or difficult to interpret may have an undiagnosed hearing problem. Again, see Appendix 1.

- While children are settling into their new environment, staff can be observing them informally in a variety of situations, focusing on the behaviours to be assessed.

- Working together wherever possible, staff complete the initial screen for each child separately.

- A behaviour should only be credited if a child is using it competently, confidently and consistently. If there is any doubt or disagreement, the behaviour should not be credited.

- The screen has three bands, and children are assessed band by band: if they do not have all the behaviours in Band 1, they do not need to be assessed on Band 2; and if they do not have all the behaviours in Band 2, they do not need to be assessed on Band 3.

- Children who lack either behaviour in Band 1 should do Getting Started instead.

- Children who have both behaviours in Band 1 but lack any of the behaviours in Band 2 are identified as Delayed, even if they have some of the behaviours in Band 3.

- Children who have all the behaviours in Bands 1 and 2 but lack any of the behaviours in Band 3 are identified as Developing.

- Children who have all the behaviours in all three bands are identified as Competent.

Skills checklist

Conversation skills uses three skills checklists to focus and guide classroom intervention and monitor individual progress:

- Early conversation skills
- Further conversation skills
- Additional conversation skills.

As these names suggest they amount to one long checklist, divided into term-sized chunks.

Each checklist consists of a number of distinct behaviours or sub-skills grouped together under a few broad types of skill. The first checklist, for example, is divided into Social contact, Listening and responding, and Taking turns. For Social contact the sub-skills are: acknowledging familiar adults and children; greeting them; and saying 'Goodbye' or something similar. It will be convenient to refer to each group of items as a skill and the different sub-skills as behaviours.

These skills and behaviours are listed in rough developmental order as a guide to intervention. Different children will of course show different patterns of development, and some of them – especially those identified as Competent – will have some or all of the behaviours already or be able to establish them almost immediately. But others may need to learn them one by one.

Children normally work through each checklist in sequence but at different speeds and with varying degrees of support, one skill at a time but usually more than one behaviour at a time. Behaviours that go together get learnt together; in working on one, staff will usually have been introducing another; and this provides an easy transition from one behaviour to the next. Some children will show some or all of the relevant behaviours already, or be able to establish them almost immediately. Others may need to learn them slowly, one by one.

Each behaviour is, however, assessed separately. Staff need to be confident that each child has established it, and the only way to be sure of that is to work through the checklists systematically, ticking them off one by one.

KEY POINTS

● Each checklist identifies three or four general skills, divided into separate behaviours or sub-skills.

● Skills and behaviours are listed in rough developmental order as a guide to intervention.

● Children normally work through each checklist in sequence, one skill at a time but usually more than one behaviour at a time.

● Every child and every behaviour needs to be assessed and monitored separately.

Classroom intervention

Conversation Skills are taught primarily through small-group work where an adult can interact closely with individual children while they are engaged in familiar activities in a familiar setting. This small-group work is supported by whole-class activities and by informal interaction with individual children during free time and daily classroom routines. Dedicated one-to-one intervention is not usually possible for all children, but can be focused on children who are slower to acquire the relevant skills as identified by the initial screen.

The checklists set specific objectives for all children on a rolling basis, while the initial screens help determine the amount of support needed for each child. Detailed advice on intervention for specific skills and behaviours is given in the Notes to each checklist.

Small-group work

Every child is assigned to a teaching group on the basis of the initial screen, possibly including, where appropriate, some mixed-ability groups: Delayed with Developing or Developing with Competent, but not Delayed with Competent, because the Competent children are likely to dominate when it is the Delayed children who need the practice. At this level it is common for children to have their own 'mother figure' or key worker who helps them settle in, plays with them, and is responsible for seeing them through the daily domestic routines. This should also be the person responsible for their small-group intervention, not just because the children will know her and be comfortable with her, but also because these routines provide many good opportunities for teaching conversation skills, and small-group work can merge easily with everyday activities.

These groups need to be kept small. 'Group work' can sometimes mean as many as ten or 12 children; for language work it should ideally be no more than six. Many children will find it difficult to understand or concentrate in a larger group. In a smaller group they can follow and join in, the teacher can relate to each child in turn, and other children in the group can learn from the exchange.

Groups also need to be kept small so staff can assess each child individually. With a larger group it is easy to think that everyone can do something when in fact some children are barely participating, if they are participating at all. Video evidence has shown, for example, that while the teacher felt that the children never stopped talking, some actually said very little or even showed much awareness of what was going on.

Each small-group teaching session should last about ten to 15 minutes. It is always better to repeat lessons than extend them. Children identified as Delayed should ideally receive at least one session day, working specifically on their conversation skills. Children identified as Developing should receive two or three sessions a week. Children identified as Competent will probably need at most one session a week but may insist on more. At this age, 'special time' with a favourite adult can be very popular.

KEY POINTS

- Children are assigned to small teaching groups on the basis of the initial screen. If possible, each group should be no more than six children, and should always work with the same adult.

- Children identified as Delayed should receive at least one small-group teaching session every day.

- Children identified as Developing should receive two or three small-group teaching sessions a week.

- Children identified as Competent should receive at least one small-group teaching session a week, for as long as they need it.

- Each teaching session should be about ten to 15 minutes long.

Whole-class work

Whole-class work is used primarily to support small-group work. Staff should try to ensure that there is at least one whole-class activity every day where they focus specifically on the skills and behaviours that their children are currently learning, especially any that are proving difficult. This does not have to be a special 'conversation' lesson; almost anything will serve, depending on the skills and behaviours in question. But two familiar classroom activities are particularly useful for teaching language skills:

● Circle games where children practise a specific skill one after another, going round the circle: for example, they take it in turns to smile and say *Hello* to the child next to them, or the teacher puts a pile of toys in the middle of the circle and the children take turns to ask the next child to fetch one. At this age, these games should be introduced first in small-group work, and only extended to larger groups or whole-class activities when all children are familiar with them.

● Talk-time where children sit and talk with their key worker about things that have happened or will happen, what they have done, the people they meet, and so on. Obviously the level will depend on how far children have got in developing conversation skills, but even a rudimentary conversation is an excellent way of reinforcing and extending children's learning.

As well as this specific focus at least once a day, almost any classroom activity can be used to support and reinforce current learning. Teacher-led activities such as playground games, art and design, PE, music and nursery rhymes can all be used to model, practise and reinforce specific skills such as responding, directing and turn-taking. This gives all children valuable experience of skills being used in different situations and contexts, with different adults, and by different children. But staff also need to be aware of any children who are finding particular skills or behaviours difficult, and be sure that they are actually following and participating, rather than letting it all go over their heads.

KEY POINTS

● There should be at least one whole-class activity every day that focuses on the skills and behaviours currently being worked on.

● The whole-class activity need not be a separate 'conversation lesson'; it can be incorporated into any familiar classroom activity.

● Other whole-class activities can also be used to support current learning, at any time, several times a day.

Informal interaction

All children should be given opportunities to practise their conversation skills several times a day. Some children get lots of conversational experience and encouragement at home; others may get very little; and we cannot always know which are which. It is important to give them all as many opportunities and as much encouragement as possible.

The suggestions for Encouraging talk in young children in Chapter 7 are still relevant here. Some of the best opportunities to use conversation to develop children's language are when they are playing, either alone or with other children. But there are many other times in the day when staff can engage children in one-to-one conversation. The daily routines of entering and leaving the classroom, putting on or taking off outdoor clothes, waiting in line, preparation and tidying up, washing and toileting, snack and meal times, all provide good opportunities for talking with children individually. Children sometimes think they are supposed to keep quiet during these activities; staff may need to make it clear that talk is not just allowed but encouraged, not just with adults but with each other.

At this level every child, especially children identified as Delayed – should have at least one personal conversation with an adult every day, to help develop their conversation skills in general. This need not always focus on the skills currently being learnt; spontaneous use of any relevant skill should be encouraged and rewarded. But it is also important to take full advantage of every opportunity where the behaviours that are currently being worked on can be modelled, encouraged and reinforced with individual children.

This is, moreover, where everyone can help. Everyone – not just classroom staff but lunchtime supervisors, playground assistants and site staff – should be encouraged to use every available opportunity to engage with these children individually. It should be part of every activity – daily routines, playground games, outings and visits – that adults talk with children about it, individually and together, before it has begun, while it is happening, and when it is finished. And not just staff: parents, grandparents and visitors (especially inspectors) too.

A list of items currently being worked on should be displayed prominently in the classroom and given to parents, so everyone can see and refer to it, and use it to guide their interaction with individual children.

KEY POINTS

- **All children, especially children identified as Delayed, should have at least one personal conversation with an adult every day.**

- **A list of the skills and behaviours currently being worked on should be displayed prominently and given to parents, so everyone can use it to guide their interaction with individual children.**

- **All staff and other adults should be encouraged to use every available opportunity to practise these skills with children individually.**

Vocabulary work

Children's development of vocabulary is crucial for their progress through school but vocabulary work is mostly an optional element in *One Step at a Time*, for reasons given in Chapter 12. For teachers who want to include systematic vocabulary work, Conversation Skills provides a list of 100 essential words selected from the vocabulary of property and relations and the vocabulary of feelings and emotion as discussed in Chapter 2. This list is intended to be supplemented with essential topic vocabulary as explained in Chapter 12.

Lesson planning

Staff may want to decide in advance what they are going to teach, when they are going to teach it, and how, so they can prepare lessons, select activities, gather resources, inform other staff, advise parents and so on. But planning also needs to be flexible because some skills may take longer to learn than expected, sometimes a lot longer, and different teaching groups will in any case be proceeding at different paces, quite apart from any children who are working on Getting Started instead of Conversation Skills.

Lesson planning includes setting objectives, selecting activities, preparing materials and allocating times. The skills checklists provide learning and teaching objectives for all children. Suggestions for appropriate activities are given in the Notes to each checklist but it should not usually be necessary to plan separate activities or prepare special materials. Staff should instead look to activities and materials they are already using, and consider how they can be used to develop the skills they have as current teaching objectives. Almost any familiar activity can be used for teaching Conversation Skills, anything that captures children's interest and encourages them to talk about it; and any special materials needed for teaching specific skills are likely to be already available in the classroom.

As well as allocating specific times for small-group or other language work, staff should also identify some activities every day where current learning can be consolidated. Similarly, longer-term planning should include some weeks when teaching groups can go back and repeat any work they have found difficult. This is particularly important for children identified as Delayed, to ensure that all learning has been properly consolidated.

Teaching method

The most effective teaching techniques are those that parents use to teach their children, usually without realising they are doing it (see Chapter 3):

● Highlighting: the adult draws attention to the behaviour by indicating it, emphasising it, or explaining when or why we do it: for example, when we should ask for help or permission, or why we should look at someone when they are speaking to us. She can do this by asking questions – 'What do we say when someone comes to visit us?', 'What can you do when you don't understand something?'; discussing the children's responses; and summarising the key points: 'So what do we do when someone comes into our classroom? We look at them, we smile, and we say "Hello"'.

- Modelling: the adult illustrates the behaviour she wants children to learn: for example, she greets each child in turn, or shows that she is listening attentively as a child speaks to her. Copying is the simplest and most natural form of learning.

- Prompting: the adult encourages the child to respond, directing him towards the appropriate behaviour by smiling, nodding or asking appropriate questions: 'Can you tell me some more about that?', 'Can I help you? What would you like me to do?', 'Did you want to ask me about that?'. If a response is not quite what she is looking for, she can encourage a more appropriate response by asking questions, prompting or modelling the skill again.

- Rewarding: the adult rewards any appropriate response with smiles, praise and further encouragement. Praise will be more effective if it can emphasise what was good about the response: 'Thank you for listening to me', 'We had a good talk together, didn't we?', 'Ah! Now I understand'. Indiscriminate praise – praising anything and everything that children say or do – does not help them to learn.

Suitable activities for teaching the various skills are suggested in the Notes to the checklists. Children may need time to get used to some of these activities. Young children do not normally understand new things – even simple stories or songs – until they have experienced them several times, so it is important to repeat new activities over at least a couple of weeks.

Monitoring progress

Continuing assessment of children's progress is crucial for effective teaching, particularly with spoken language where it is so easy to overestimate children's abilities, or move them on before learning has been properly consolidated. Many – perhaps most – will already have the early behaviours in Checklist 1. But some may not, and the only way of knowing for sure which is which, and exactly which behaviours they do have, is by observing each child individually.

This need not be as onerous and time-consuming as it seems. The checklists provide a quick and simple way of recording individual progress. As each child exhibits a behaviour confidently, competently and consistently, it is ticked off on the checklist. This should not be on the basis of a single occasion. Each behaviour needs to be consistent – repeated and reliable – as well as confident and competent.

Staff may want to wait until the end of the week before reviewing all the children in their group and bringing the checklists up to date. The best test is whether children are showing a behaviour spontaneously, outside of small-group teaching. Behaviour should not be assessed on the basis of small-group work alone, and if there is any doubt about a particular behaviour it should not be credited. It is always better to underestimate children's abilities than overestimate them.

Staff also need to be sure that children are not just demonstrating that behaviour as a result of the week's teaching but have properly consolidated it. There can be considerable variation, from child to child and from skill to skill, in how long it takes to consolidate new learning. Most children consolidate new skills easily and naturally through normal classroom experience, but those who are slow to establish a skill in the first place are also likely to need longer to consolidate it. It can be useful to have some way of noting behaviours that are uncertain or inconsistent as well as those that seem to be firmly established, by, for example, using one tick for a skill that is hesitant or inconsistent and two ticks for one that is firmly established. Staff can then use this to gauge how long it takes each child to consolidate a behaviour, and whether some forms of intervention are proving more effective than others.

Staff should also make a note of any behaviours that have proved difficult so they can go over them again later in the term, and should allow time for this in their long-term planning. They may need to come back to some of them several times, especially with children in the Delayed group. They should also allow a couple of weeks at the beginning of each term to check the previous term's learning; and then repeat teaching of any items that children seem to have forgotten. It is always more important that children consolidate basic skills than that they move on to more advanced ones.

KEY POINTS

- Each child is monitored separately using the checklists. As each child acquires a behaviour it is ticked off on the checklist.

- A behaviour should only be credited when the child is using it confidently, competently and consistently. If there is any doubt about a behaviour, it should not be credited.

- Staff need to ensure that each behaviour has been properly consolidated, and should return later to any items that have proved difficult, to confirm that previous learning has been retained.

- It is always more important that children consolidate basic skills than that they move on to more advanced ones.

Moving on

In general, each group keeps working on the same few behaviours until everyone in that group has learnt them. Then they move on to the next few behaviours or the next skill, and so on through the checklist. Each group can work at its own pace but the pace of the group as a whole should always be geared to its slower members. It does not matter if some children are learning more quickly than others. It is always better to consolidate than push ahead too soon; all children will benefit from the extra practice; and if some of them can do some things comfortably, the others may be able to learn from them.

Early-years staff sometimes think they need to keep changing material or activities to retain children's interest and extend their experience, but, as every parent knows, young children like to repeat things over and over again: the same stories, the same songs, the same little phrases, the same little routines, day after day. Children under five will always benefit from repeating activities, particularly if they are having difficulty with the language that goes with them.

There may however come a time when a group just has to move on, because some children are becoming bored or frustrated, or are showing signs of stress or anxiety at the constant repetition. This might be a good time to reorganise teaching groups, or a group can come back again to the same items later on, by which time the children having difficulty may be more ready for them. It is a good idea in any case to repeat any items that have proved difficult, as a way of reinforcing and consolidating everyone's learning as well as providing further support for those who need it.

It may also be convenient to keep the class more or less together. Intervention needs to be differentiated, to meet the needs of different children, but it also needs to be manageable. If one group has completed a particular skill, staff can mark time with them while they give more attention to the other groups that are still working on it. Alternatively, they can let each group move on to the next skill as soon as they are ready, but this will mean that different groups are working on different skills, and that some groups may complete the checklist well before others.

Either way, it is much easier to manage if the class is working on only one checklist at a time. Staff should continue working on the same checklist until everyone – or almost everyone – has completed it. There may still be some children who are simply not ready to move on with the rest. They really need to keep working on the same few behaviours, but if they do they will only fall further and further behind. Depending on resources, it may be possible to keep them together for specialist small-group work, or provide some additional personal support.

Each checklist is expected to take about a term to complete but, allowing for the time needed for initial screening at the beginning of the year and for any preliminary work on Getting Started, it may not be possible to complete all three checklists within a school year. In any case, the skills in Checklist 3 may be too advanced for some children. But what matters more than how far anyone gets is that everyone acquires the more basic skills before being expected to master more advanced ones.

It is, however, impossible to be precise about any of this. One size is not going to fit all, and staff will need to use their own experience and judgement in deciding when and how to move on from one behaviour, skill or checklist to the next.

Links to literacy

Literacy is essentially the skill of turning unfamiliar written marks into familiar sounds or thoughts (reading) or turning those sounds or thoughts into marks (writing). The sounds and thoughts come first. Spoken language comes before written language, in both individual development and the development of cultures. Learning to read and write is like learning a second language, something that some people find harder than others.

If children are to read or write fluently they first need to be fluent in their original language: spoken language. For reading, they need to have a good understanding of spoken words and sentences, to enable them to follow the meaning while they concentrate on decoding the written script. The larger their vocabulary the more likely they will be familiar with both the sound patterns and the meanings of the words they meet in their reading. This will help them guess what a written word might mean from its opening sounds and/or its context. Similarly, familiarity with the way words group together to form sentences helps children anticipate and predict both words and meanings.

For writing, they need to be able to express themselves, to know how to say what they want to say, while they concentrate on making the written marks. The larger their vocabulary and the more confident and competent they are in talking, the easier they will find it to write at any length.

The easiest, most basic, most natural way in which children develop this fluency is through conversation, by talking with adults and other children. The conversational abilities developed at this level of the programme are an essential – perhaps *the* essential – pre-literacy skill. Conversation helps children expand their vocabulary and extend the structure of their sentences; it adds to the content of what they can talk and think about; and since it requires listening as well as speaking it increases their understanding.

At the same time, children should be developing other pre-literacy and literacy-support skills, including:

- Awareness and understanding of reading: By this age children ought to be becoming aware of the nature and function of reading, by enjoying stories that are read to them, and looking at and talking about picture books. Ideally, all children would be familiar with stories and nursery rhymes from their earliest years but this does not always happen, and ensuring that they all have this experience is an essential part of pre-school education.

- Auditory and phonic skills: Listening skills become increasingly important as children begin to learn to read, when they will need to be able to identify the sounds in words and relate them to the written marks. In *One Step at a Time* these skills are promoted at the next level of the programme when they become more relevant but the foundations need to be laid before then, from hearing and learning simple nursery songs and rhymes. Nursery rhymes, and in particular learning and enjoying the rhyming words, helps children 'tune-in' to the sounds of words. Learning to march or clap in time to music helps them 'tune-in' to the rhythm of sounds, which will later be important in recognising syllable structure and the shape of sentences for spelling and writing.

- Visual-motor skills: These are important for writing, when children need to be able to recognise and form the different letter shapes. They can be developed even at this age by using form boards or other toys that require children to choose things by shape and fit them to holes; by learning to handle simple craft tools like paintbrushes, crayons, scissors and glue sticks; and by attempting to draw or colour in simple shapes.

- Awareness, understanding and use of writing: By this age children ought also to be becoming aware of the purpose of writing and its different uses: signs, labels, lists, greetings cards, and so on, as well as books and magazines. They should also be showing an interest in the act of writing, particularly when an adult writes their name for them on a label or in a birthday card, and may even want to try it themselves by scribbling with a pen or pencil.

Child's name	Band 1	Is talking frequently and spontaneously to adults or other children	Is joining words together in most of their utterances	Band 2	When in a group, attends to person speaking, e.g. looks, listens, shows interest	Responds verbally to comments or questions	Band 3	Asks for help if needed	Initiates conversation appropriately with different adults and children	*Competent*	*Developing*	*Delayed*
_____												
_____												
_____												
_____												
_____												
_____												
_____												
_____												
_____												
_____												
_____												
_____												
_____												
_____												
_____												
_____												
_____												

- Children who lack either of the behaviours in Band 1 should do *Getting Started* before doing Conversation Skills.

- Children who have the behaviours in Band 1 but lack any of the behaviours in Band 2 are identified as *Delayed*, even if they have some of the behaviours in Band 3.

- Children who have all the behaviours in Bands 1 and 2 but lack any of the behaviours in Band 3 are identified as *Developing*.

- Children who have all the behaviours in all three Bands are identified as *Competent*.

Teaching Speaking and Listening © Ann Locke (Bloomsbury Publishing plc, 2013)

Teaching Speaking and Listening © Ann Locke (Bloomsbury Publishing plc, 2013)

Child's name

Social contact

											Acknowledges familiar adults and children, e.g. looks or smiles
											Greets familiar adults and children, e.g. says 'Hello'
											Says 'Goodbye' (or similar) to familiar adults and children

Listening and responding

											When in a group, attends to person speaking, e.g. looks, listens, shows interest
											Responds to instructions appropriately
											Responds non-verbally to comments or questions, e.g. nods or shakes head
											Replies to comments or questions
											Comments on what other people have said

Taking turns

											Takes turns in games and nursery routines
											Can play passing on an object or message
											Waits for turn in games or circle activities
											Allows others to speak (waits for turn in conversation)

Teaching Speaking and Listening © Ann Locke (Bloomsbury Publishing plc, 2013)

Child's name

Expressing needs and wants

											Can ask for help or permission when needed
											Can say or ask when wants or needs something
											Can say or ask when wants someone else to do something

Initiating conversation

											Can initiate a conversation non-verbally, e.g. by holding up or pointing to something
											Can initiate a conversation verbally, by commenting on something
											Can initiate a conversation by asking a question

Maintaining conversation

											Can continue a conversation by commenting on what has been said
											Can continue a conversation by asking question
											Can give an extended response (at least two sentences)
											Can maintain a conversation for at least three turns per person

Conversation in everyday routines

											Regularly converses when dressing or undressing
											Regularly converses when eating or drinking
											Regularly converses when toileting or washing
											Regularly converses when playing with other children

Child's name

Describing needs, wants and feelings

												Can talk about their current needs and wants
												Can talk about their feelings

Understanding reasons

												Will respond to reasons why or why not
												Can give simple reasons why or why not

Conversational etiquette

												Does not talk when others are talking
												Does not terminate conversations inappropriately, e.g. if someone else is speaking
												Uses some social language spontaneously, e.g. 'Hullo', ''Bye', 'Thanks', 'Can I…?'

Clarifying

												Indicates if hasn't understood, e.g. by asking a question
												Will try to explain if asked, but may just repeat the same words
												Will try to explain if asked, using different words
												Recognises when others haven't understood them

Vocabulary wordlist

Conversation Skills

Quality	Colour	Texture	Sound	Shape	Size	Quantity	Number	Space	Time	Movement	Feelings and emotion
dirty	black	cold	loud	circle	big	a bit	first	behind	after	away	clever
easy	blue	dry	noisy	dot/spot	biggest	a lot	last	by	bedtime	backwards	frightened
empty	colour	hard	quiet	flat	little	as many	number	down	again	fast	funny
full	green	hot	sound	line	long	as much		in	birthday	go	good
heavy	red	soft		round	small	all		in front of	clock	move	happy
like	yellow	wet		straight	smallest	another (one)		inside	daytime	quick	hungry
new				square		any		near	soon	shake	kind
						many		next to		slow	naughty
						more		on		start	nice
						no more		on top of		stop	sad
						some		off		still	pretty
								out		through	silly
								outside			sorry
								over			thirsty
								to			
								under			
								up			

Teaching Speaking and Listening © Ann Locke (Bloomsbury Publishing plc, 2013)

NOTES ON CHECKLIST 1

Early conversation skills

This checklist features the early skills, some of them pre-verbal, that children need if they are to become competent conversationalists. Some of these skills are elementary and many children will have them already, but they may need to be taught and practised with some children.

Social contact

Knowing how to approach other people and make contact with them in an acceptable way is an important social skill and a foundation of conversation first with friends and familiar adults, then with less familiar adults. Some children may have to learn how to do this, using the behaviour of staff as a model.

These skills are most usefully taught in the context of daily classroom routines, especially at the beginning and end of the day, or through circle games, for example with children taking it in turns to saying 'Hello' or 'Goodbye'.

Listening and responding

Young children do not always recognise when an adult is talking to them; it literally goes over their heads. They may have to learn to attend, take in what is said, and show that they have understood.

Showing that you are listening by looking at the speaker or nodding your head is an important conversational skill. It can be very off-putting if someone you are talking to fails to respond in any way, and the conversation quickly breaks down.

Staff can use talk-time to explain to children why it is important to listen, and how they should respond to indicate they have heard and understood. They can then encourage and highlight the appropriate responses. Circle games can also be used to practise these skills, for example: Following directions, where each child in turn gives his neighbour an instruction such as 'Give a blue brick to Patti' (from a box of coloured bricks in the middle of the circle); or Answering questions, where each child in turn asks his neighbour a question such as 'What's your name?' or 'Where is the....?'.

Taking turns

Turn-taking is an important social skill in all sorts of situations, not just in conversation. Children need to learn to wait their turn in any number of classroom and playground activities as well as learning how to take turns in conversation, as speaker and as listener. Taking turns in play helps give them an understanding of this procedure. They also need to learn the cues through which we signal our readiness to switch roles from listener to speaker and back again. Some basic turn-taking skills are included in the Getting Started programme and can also be used here.

Staff can use talk-time to discuss why turn-taking matters in general, for example when playing with toys or when asking the teacher questions, and why it is important to listen and wait their turn in a conversation. Turn-taking in conversation can then be practised in talk-time and circle-time, as well as in daily routines.

NOTES ON CHECKLIST 2

Further conversational skills

This checklist includes the minimum skills that children need to engage in simple conversations.

Expressing needs and wants

Many children will indicate non-verbally when they need help or want something, for example by pointing, grunting, or tugging at an adult. They need to learn how to use talk to make their needs and wants known, not only as a social skill – pointing and grunting is not normally considered acceptable – but because it is a more accurate and effective way of getting things done. This includes asking for help or permission, for example to go to the toilet, saying or asking when they want something ('Can I have the scissors?', 'Can I do some cutting?'), and saying or asking when they want others to do something for them ('Can you read me a story?').

Staff can use talk-time to discuss with children the ways they sometimes need help, and how they can ask for it. Where children are not expressing themselves verbally, staff can help either directly, by highlighting the skill in question ('Remember how we ask for something'), or indirectly, by putting the question to the child, asking it for him ('Do you need help with your coat? Shall I help take it off?').

Initiating conversation

As well as responding to an adult's conversational moves, children also need to be able to initiate conversations themselves, with familiar adults and with other children. This takes a certain amount of self-confidence, so it needs to be built on a warm and friendly relationship with each child.

If an adult has the child's confidence he will normally start initiating conversations spontaneously, but some children can be slow to develop this skill. Frequent conversation initiated by an adult will help. Commenting on your own experience ('Wasn't it a lovely weekend? I sat in my back garden reading a book.') can be more effective in getting children to talk than asking questions. But be prepared to be patient: it is important not to rush or push the child. It is virtually impossible to get children to talk if they don't want to!

Maintaining conversation

A conversation is more than just one or two exchanges between speakers. It requires a series of exchanges, with different people taking turns as speaker. Responses need to be appropriate and sensitively timed; a response that it is too quick or too slow can interfere with the flow of a conversation as surely as a failure to respond at all.

Staff can help children maintain a conversation by showing interest, commenting on what the child is saying, or asking questions that are within his capacity to answer. Open questions are better for stimulating conversation than closed yes/no questions or test questions (questions with a determinate answer), for example 'What a nice picture! Can you tell me about it?' rather than 'What is it?'. At the end of any conversation staff should highlight and praise the child's contribution: 'That was interesting. I liked talking about your dog'. They should also comment on and praise any instances of children talking to each other: 'I saw you had a nice talk with Mary'.

Conversation in everyday routines

Children need to be able to use conversation in many different contexts, not just the situations where staff have been teaching conversation skills. Conversation occurs most easily in situations that are familiar and involving. At this age these will be the daily domestic and classroom routines, so these will be the situations where children have most to talk about and will find it easiest to talk.

Children should not be credited with these items unless they are conversing competently and confidently, frequently and freely, in the appropriate contexts. The crucial thing is the amount of conversation, not its accuracy or adequacy.

NOTES ON CHECKLIST 3

Additional conversation skills

This checklist features more sophisticated conversation skills that normally take a long time to develop and will be present only in an elementary form at this age. They are quite subtle and need to be introduced slowly and carefully. It does not matter if children do not master all the skills on this checklist. Terminating a conversation and clarifying are likely to be particularly difficult and it may only be possible to introduce the general idea, explaining it, and why it is important, without expecting children to demonstrate the skill. Some more sophisticated skills like being able to keep to a topic, or moving smoothly from one topic to another, are not included because children tend not to develop them until later.

Describing needs, wants and feelings

Being able to recognise their own and other people's feelings is an essential social skill that children need if they are to cope with the complex demands of school life and other social interactions. Learning to describe their needs, wants and feelings as well as express them introduces them to the vocabulary of emotion and helps them understand what needs, wants and feelings are.

Staff can use talk-time to talk about the feelings that arise in different everyday situations and get children to talk about when they might feel happy or sad, or what makes them feel frightened or sorry. They can also use story-time to highlight and discuss the feelings of characters in a story. This is the best way to handle talk about negative emotions that children may find difficult or worrying.

Understanding reasons

Being able to solve problems and negotiate behaviour through talk rather than conflict is another important social – and classroom – skill. Learning how to reason and resolve conflicts through discussion takes many years. But as a first step, children need to recognise that others have needs, wants and feelings of their own, and understand their reasons when they want others to do or not to do various things.

Staff can use story-time or talk-time to discuss how different people might have different wants, needs or feelings in the same situation, or how they might want different outcomes. Story-time can also be used to discuss the reasons why the characters might want to do something, or might not want something to happen. Children's responses to questions about the characters' motivations will show if they have a grasp of their reasons for actions. They can then be asked about the reasons for their own actions, why they want certain things to happen or not happen, and whether these reasons apply to everyone or will be accepted by others. The reasons they provide may not always fit with adult thinking – and are sometimes quite bizarre – but still need to be taken seriously.

Conversational etiquette

Conversational etiquette isn't just politeness, it's an important part of knowing how to relate to other people, especially unfamiliar people. Someone who is abrupt or awkward in their conversation quickly makes other people feel uncomfortable. Children are less likely to notice these things than adults, and will need to learn the little niceties that put other people at ease.

These skills include not interrupting when others are talking and waiting until a conversation is finished, not just turning away or walking off while someone is still talking. If this does happen, it is an opportunity to explain why it is inappropriate and what the appropriate behaviour would be: 'Wait a minute, Jason, I'm still talking. You should wait until I've finished'. Staff can also model these skills by making it clear when it's someone else's turn, or when a conversation has ended: 'Now tell me what you did'; 'That was good, but now I need to talk with Saad'.

Social language like 'Please' or 'Thanks', or 'Can I have…?' instead of 'I want…', are sometimes referred to as 'social oil' because they smooth the path of a conversation.

Similarly, children need to be able to keep to the topic without going off at tangents which confuse other people or prevent them from saying things they still wanted to say.

Clarifying

Children also need to grasp how conversations can break down through failure to understand and how they can be repaired. This comes in stages: they need to be able to recognise when they haven't understood something, and have the confidence to ask or say so; and they need to recognise when others haven't understood them, and be able to expand what they said or explain what they mean. This last point is a more sophisticated skill that they may not develop at this stage, but they should at least be able to respond appropriately when asked to explain, even if all they can do is repeat the same words.

Staff can use talk-time to explain that we don't always understand what other people are saying. It is important to stress it doesn't matter, not anyone's fault, and it's alright to ask for more information: 'If you're not sure what I said, you can just put up your hand and ask'. They can also model uncertainty, verbally and non-verbally, and praise any similar response from the child: 'That was sensible, asking me to say it again'. If a child fails to give the appropriate response, staff can encourage him with leading questions like 'Can you remember all that?', 'Did you follow what I said?', 'Would you like me to say it again?'.

Staff can also use talk-time to explain that we don't always make ourselves clear, and that we sometimes need to explain when others haven't understood. They should also find or create opportunities to model repair: 'I didn't explain that very well. Let me try again'. They should also ask children for clarification whenever appropriate, using language that will help the child respond appropriately: 'I'm still not sure what happened. Can you tell me again?'. Note that at this stage the relevant behaviour is being able to expand or explain if asked, not that children do this spontaneously when others haven't understood them.

Chapter 9 Listening Skills

Listening Skills is a programme for developing children's phonic skills and their understanding of spoken language, in preparation for reading and other demands of the early school curriculum. It is intended for children aged four to five who have previously done Conversation Skills. If a significant number of children have not had this experience it is recommended that the whole class does some Conversation Skills work before commencing Listening Skills. Listening Skills is expected to take about a year to complete but it is more important that children consolidate basic skills than that they finish this level of the programme.

Listening is a complex skill. It includes hearing, attending, understanding and remembering. Children begin to develop these skills from an early age, not just in conversation but also from listening to songs, rhymes and stories, and listening to talk about pictures and stories as well as about the things around them. Children who have not had these experiences may lack these skills. Some may have poor hearing that has not been identified. Others may have difficulty attending, understanding or remembering. Others – especially if they have been doing Conversation Skills – may have to learn to stop talking and start listening!

The most fundamental skill that children need at school is the ability to understand basic classroom language. They have to understand simple questions and follow simple directions and instructions if they are to learn anything at all – or even survive! – in the classroom. They also need to be able to hear the difference between different syllables and word sounds if they are to grasp phonics and use them for reading, writing and spelling. But children also need to learn a different type of listening from the listening they are used to at home.

Most listening at home is listening to conversations on familiar topics and between familiar people. They speak directly to each other and children can take part as appropriate. This conversational listening continues in pre-school and at school in small-group or one-to-one teaching, but most listening at school is very different. At school, adults talk to a group or a class as well as to individuals. They may even be unfamiliar adults talking about unfamiliar things. Children may also be at a distance from the person who is speaking, sitting while the speaker is standing, in a large space, and with any number of other children. Without the direct eye contact they are used to, they may not even realise that all this talk is intended for them.

On top of all that, talk may be about things that happened hours, days or weeks ago, or things that haven't happened yet. Children may have to remember what was said some considerable time before ('Does everyone remember what we talked about yesterday?'). And they will also have to learn to listen for much longer periods than they are used to (extended listening), without responding until they're told to ('Quiet now! Sit still and listen.'). It is a different, more intensive and more focused, type of listening that children are going to need to acquire at school, and some of them will find it very difficult.

Children will normally develop extended listening from hearing bedtime or other stories, starting with simple picture books and building up to detailed narratives. Children who lack this experience may have difficulty not just in attending for any length of time but with following a story, or even the very idea of a narrative where a series of events follow one another. Television is no substitute because the programmes (and the adverts!) are typically episodic, relying on exciting incidents to hold children's attention rather than a story line, if indeed there is one. If children seem bored, distracted or naughty during story-time – or even if they are sitting quietly and passively – it may be because they simply do not understand why the teacher keeps on talking all the time.

Moreover, understanding a story or factual account usually involves more than understanding what is actually written or said (explicit or surface meaning); we also have to be able to read or listen 'between the lines' (implicit or contextual meaning). We normally have to add a great deal of background knowledge and personal experience about the world and the way it works, and about people and the way they work. Storytelling or any sort of description, spoken or written, would be impossible if we had to be precise and explicit about everything, in the way we sometimes do have to explain everything to very young children. By this age, children need to be able to work many things out for themselves.

One particularly important form of this understanding is recognising why the characters in a story behave as they do, what they are feeling, and why they are feeling it, all of which is often left implicit. It usually gets taken for granted that children will understand why a character is angry or sad, crying or running away. But teachers who ask their class – or, preferably, a small group – 'Why was the boy crying?' or 'Why did the girl get angry?' may be surprised at some of the answers. This type of understanding is obviously important for children's social and emotional development and their understanding of their own and other people's feelings and behaviour. But it is also needed for curriculum subjects like early science: for example, understanding why some animals come out at night or live in trees.

All these listening skills impact on literacy. Children need to be able to recognise sound patterns so they can use sound-letter links for reading, writing and spelling, but other listening skills are also crucial. The better children's understanding of spoken language, the better their reading comprehension and the more they will learn from what they read. Extended listening also prepares them for extended writing. Even understanding a range of question forms helps them to understand what they are reading and know what to write, or at least helps them to find out.

Listening Skills is primarily intended for children aged four to five who have already done Conversation Skills. In a class where a significant number of children have not had this experience, it is recommended that they all have some practice with Conversation Skills first, before beginning Listening Skills. How much work they will need on Conversation Skills will depend on their ability and confidence but they should at least work through the second checklist.

Children who have completed Listening Skills should be well prepared for the more formal types of learning that they will meet in later years. They will be familiar with group listening, and able to follow directions and instructions, answer questions, and follow lengthy accounts and explanations. They will have the foundations for literacy, especially reading: they will enjoy listening to and learning stories, songs and rhymes; they will recognise how sounds are used to form and spell out words; and they will be able to follow, interpret and learn from both stories and factual accounts.

Initial screening

The initial screen helps staff:

- 'tune-in' to the relevant skills at this level of the programme
- identify children's current development of these skills
- determine the amount of support they are likely to need.

The first of these may be the most important. For Listening Skills staff need to be particularly aware of children's level of understanding, the extent to which they grasp the meaning of what is being said to them, and of their ability to discriminate and identify different sounds, in particular the sounds that make up the English language.

They also need to be aware of the differences in these skills between children, so they can provide the targeted support that is needed. Which children pay attention? Respond readily? Look confused? Know songs and rhymes, without following other children? Recognise rhymes or other sounds?

All this can be more difficult than it might seem. Staff may not be used to discriminating these behaviours, or identifying them in individual children. These are the skills they need to develop, and the screening process can help them do it.

The initial screen is a quick and simple measure of current development, not a formal assessment. It identifies children as:

- Competent: they seem to be acquiring these skills without too much difficulty and are not expected to need special attention.
- Developing: they seem to be slower in acquiring these skills and are likely to need some support and attention.
- Delayed: they seem to be having difficulty in acquiring these skills and are likely to need more intensive support and attention.

These groupings are intended to be flexible and are likely to change in the course of a term or year.

Screening should not be carried out until children have settled into their new class and become used to their new environment. This may take weeks or even months, especially if children have just started school. But it does give staff time to observe all children informally in a variety of situations, focusing on the skills to be assessed.

The screen can then be completed, working with a colleague if possible. Children's behaviour can be variable at this age and a second opinion is always useful. It is also easy to take some of these behaviours for granted, or underestimate the skills of quiet children and overestimate the skills of more talkative ones.

Each child needs to be considered separately. Staff are often surprised to discover that while it seems 'the whole class' can do something, there are actually huge variations in what individual children contribute, and their level of detail or accuracy, with some of them barely understanding what the task is.

It is also important to consider each behaviour separately. A behaviour should only be credited if a child is using it confidently, competently and consistently. If there is any doubt or disagreement, the behaviour should not be credited. It is always better to underestimate children's abilities than overestimate them.

The initial screen has two bands, and children are assessed band by band. That is, if they do not have all the behaviours in Band 1, they do not need to be assessed on Band 2.

● Children who lack any of the behaviours in Band 1 are identified as Delayed, even if they have some of the behaviours in Band 2.

● Children who have all the behaviours in Band 1 but lack any of the behaviours in Band 2 are identified as Developing.

● Children who have all the behaviours in both bands are identified as Competent.

The Delayed group may include some children with special educational needs but should not be thought of as a special needs group. Children can be delayed for all sorts of reasons, including lack of confidence, lack of experience, or lack of familiarity with the English language; and some children with special needs may have perfectly adequate listening skills, or show uneven patterns of development. Children with special needs may need extra support but should be included in the *One Step* programme in the same way as any other child. For further guidance see Appendix 1.

Children whose listening skills seem delayed or whose speech is unclear or jumbled may have an undiagnosed hearing problem or a specific language difficulty. Again, see Appendix 1.

- While children are settling into their new class, staff can be observing them informally in a variety of situations, focusing on the behaviours to be assessed.

- Working with a colleague if possible, staff complete the initial screen for each child separately.

- A behaviour should be credited only if a child is using it competently, confidently and consistently. If there is any doubt or disagreement, the behaviour should not be credited.

- The screen has two bands, and children are assessed band by band. If they do not have all the behaviours in Band 1, they do not need to be assessed on Band 2.

- Children who lack any of the behaviours in Band 1 are identified as Delayed, even if they have some of the behaviours in Band 2.

- Children who have all the behaviours in Band 1 but lack any of the behaviours in Band 2 are identified as Developing

- Children who have all the behaviours in both bands are identified as Competent.

Skills checklists

Listening Skills uses three skills checklists to focus and guide classroom intervention and monitor individual progress:

- Understanding instructions and questions

- Hearing sound and word patterns

- Understanding meaning.

Each checklist consists of a number of distinct behaviours or sub-skills grouped together under a few broad types of skill. The first checklist, for example, is divided into Following instructions, Early question forms and Later question forms (a question form is a general type of question like 'What is …? or 'Who can …?'). For Following instructions, for example, the sub-skills range from following a single simple instruction to following a complex sequence of instructions. It will be convenient to refer to each group of items as a skill and the separate items as behaviours.

These skills, behaviours and question forms are listed in rough developmental order as a guide to intervention. Different children will of course show different patterns of development, and some of them – especially those identified as Competent – will have some or all of the behaviours already or be able to establish them almost immediately. But others may need to learn them one by one.

Children normally work through each checklist in sequence but at different speeds and with varying degrees of support, usually one skill at a time. With Listening Skills, however, the question forms in Checklist 1 can run in parallel with Following instructions, and also, if necessary, overlap with Checklist 2: that is, the class should start with Following instructions but the first question forms can be introduced as soon as the class is ready. However, each group of question forms is best worked on separately: that is, children should not start work on the later question forms until they have learnt all the earlier ones.

Children will, moreover, usually be working on more than one behaviour or question form at a time. Items that go together get learnt together; in working on one, staff will usually have been introducing another; and this provides an easy transition from one item to the next. Some children will show some or all of the relevant behaviours already, or be able to establish them almost immediately. Others may need to learn them slowly, one by one.

Each behaviour is, however, assessed separately. Staff need to be confident that each child has established it, and the only way to be sure of that is to work through the checklists systematically, ticking them off one by one.

KEY POINTS

- Each checklist identifies three or four general skills, divided into separate behaviours or question forms.

- Skills and behaviours are listed in rough developmental order as a guide to intervention.

- Children normally work through each checklist in sequence, one skill at a time, but the question forms in Checklist 1 can run in parallel with Following instructions or Checklist 2.

- Teaching of different behaviours and question forms will usually overlap.

- Every child and every behaviour needs to be assessed and monitored separately.

Classroom intervention

Listening Skills are taught primarily through small-group work supported by whole-class activities and informal interaction during free time and daily classroom routines. The checklists set specific objectives for all children on a rolling basis, while the initial screens help determine the amount of support needed for each child. Detailed advice on intervention for specific skills and behaviours is given in the Notes to each checklist.

Small-group work

Every child is assigned to a teaching group on the basis of the initial screen, possibly including, where appropriate, some mixed-ability groups: Delayed with Developing or Developing with Competent, but not Delayed with Competent, because the Competent children are likely to dominate when it is the Delayed children who need the practice.

These groups need to be kept small. 'Group work' can sometimes mean as many as ten or 12 children; for listening work it should ideally be no more than six. Many children will find it difficult to understand or concentrate in a larger group. In a smaller group they can follow and join in, the teacher can relate to each child in turn, and other children in the group can learn from the exchange.

Groups also need to be kept small so staff can assess each child individually. With a larger group it is easy to think that everyone can do something when in fact some children are barely participating, if they are participating at all. Video evidence has shown, for example, that while the teacher felt that the children never stopped talking, some actually said very little or even showed much awareness of what was going on.

Small-group work on listening skills, especially the phonic skills in the second checklist, needs to be in a quiet area – outside the main classroom, if at all possible – where children will not be distracted or disturbed. Background noise or activity will make it difficult for children to concentrate and listen.

Each small-group session should last 15 to 20 minutes. It is always better to repeat lessons than extend them. Children identified as Delayed should ideally receive at least one session a day, working specifically on their listening skills. Children identified as Developing should receive two or three sessions a week. Children identified as Competent will probably need at most one session a week but may nevertheless insist on having their own special time to play 'listening games' with a favourite adult.

KEY POINTS

- Children are assigned to small teaching groups on the basis of the initial screen. If possible, each group should be no more than six children and should always work with the same adult.

- Children identified as Delayed should receive at least one small-group teaching session every day.

- Children identified as Developing should receive two or three small-group teaching sessions a week.

- Children identified as Competent should receive at least one small-group teaching session a week, for as long as they need it.

- Each teaching session should be 15 to 20 minutes long.

Whole-class work

Whole-class work is used to teach question forms (Checklist 1) and nursery rhymes (Checklist 2), and to reinforce and consolidate small-group skills work. For advice on question forms and nursery rhymes see the Notes to the checklists.

To support small-group skills work, staff should try to ensure that there is at least one whole-class activity every day where they focus specifically on any skills and behaviours that children are currently learning, especially those that are proving difficult. This does not have to be a special 'listening' lesson; almost anything will serve, depending on the skills and behaviours in question. But two familiar classroom activities are particularly useful for teaching listening skills:

● Circle games, where children practise a specific skill one after another, going round the circle. For example, there is a pile of toys or a set of pictures in the middle of the circle, and each child in turn gives the next child an instruction or asks a question.

● Talking partners, where children talk with each other in pairs. For example, the teacher gives everyone an instruction and one child has to explain to the other what it is they have to do. Then she gives another instruction, and it's the turn of the other child to explain it.

These may need to be introduced in small-group work first and only extended to a whole-class or large-group activity when children are comfortable with them.

As well as this specific focus on listening skills at least once a day, almost any classroom activity can be used to support and reinforce current learning, at any time, several times a day. Things like giving and following instructions, asking and answering questions, and conveying and understanding meaning are fundamental to all teaching and belong in any lesson; classroom routines like clearing up or getting ready to go outdoors can be used for work on instructions and questions; a few spare minutes before break can be used to practise nursery rhymes; and so on. This gives all children valuable experience of skills being used in different situations and contexts, with different adults, and by different children. But staff also need to be aware of any children who are finding particular skills or behaviours difficult, and be sure that they are actually following and participating, rather than letting it all go over their heads.

Informal interaction

All children should be given opportunities to practise their listening skills several times a day. There are many other times in the day when staff can engage with children one-to-one. The daily routines of entering and leaving the classroom, putting on or taking off outdoor clothes, waiting in line, preparation and tidying up, washing and toileting, snack and meal times, all provide good opportunities for practising question forms and other skills with individual children. Most of the behaviours in Checklists 2 and 3 need specific materials or activities, but others – like reciting a nursery rhyme – can be practised at any time.

This is, moreover, where everyone can help. All children should have at least one personal conversation with an adult every day, and everyone in the school – not just teachers and classroom assistants but lunchtime supervisors, playground assistants and site staff – has a role to play. It should be part of everyone's job description that they talk with children – not to them or at them but with them – whenever and wherever possible. It should be part of every school activity – daily routines, lessons, outings and visits – that adults talk with children about them, individually and together, before it has begun, while it is happening, and when it is finished. And not just staff: parents, grandparents and visitors (especially inspectors) too.

A list of items currently being worked on should be displayed prominently in the classroom and given to parents, so everyone can see and refer to it, and use it to guide their interaction with individual children.

Vocabulary work

Children's development of vocabulary is crucial for their progress through school but vocabulary work is mostly an optional element in *One Step at a Time*, for reasons given in Chapter 12. For teachers who want to include systematic vocabulary work, Listening Skills provides a list of 100 essential words selected from the vocabulary of property and relations and the vocabulary of feelings and emotion as discussed in Chapter 2. This list is intended to be supplemented with essential topic vocabulary as explained in Chapter 12.

Lesson planning

Staff may want to decide in advance what they are going to teach, when they are going to teach it, and how, so they can prepare lessons, select activities, gather resources, inform other staff, advise parents and so on. But planning also needs to be flexible because some skills may take longer to learn than expected, sometimes very much longer, and different teaching groups will in any case be proceeding at different paces.

Lesson planning includes setting objectives, selecting activities, preparing materials and allocating times. The skills checklists provide learning and teaching objectives for all children. Suggestions for appropriate activities are given in the Notes to each checklist but it should not usually be necessary to plan separate activities or prepare special materials. Staff should instead look to activities and materials they are already using, and consider how they can be used to develop the skills they have as current teaching objectives. Almost any activity can be used for teaching Checklists 1 and 3, but Checklist 2 will require specialist material, some of which may already be available in an existing phonics programme.

As well as allocating specific times for small-group or other language work, staff should also identify some activities every day where current learning can be consolidated. Similarly, longer-term planning should include some weeks when teaching groups can go back and repeat any work they have found difficult. This is particularly important for children identified as Delayed, to ensure that all learning has been properly consolidated.

Teaching method

Teaching listening skills is not difficult but it does need time and attention. The more limited children's experience at home – if, for example, they are not familiar with nursery rhymes or have not had regular bedtime stories – the more support they will need at school. Repetition is particularly important but at this age children positively enjoy repeating songs and rhymes, day after day, week after week, and the same story can be told every day for at least a week without them becoming bored. Indeed, it may not be until the third, fourth, or even fifth time that some of them begin to understand it. Rhymes and songs can take even longer.

The most effective teaching techniques are those that parents use to teach their children, usually without realising they are doing it (see Chapter 3):

● Highlighting: the teacher draws attention to the relevant behaviour by discussing it, explaining its importance, or explaining how, when or why we do it: for example, when and why we need to listen carefully, or why it is difficult to follow a two-part instruction. She can also do this by asking questions – 'How do we find a rhyming word?' – and discussing the responses, then summarising and highlighting the key points: 'We listen to all the words and try to find ones that sound the same at the end'.

● Modelling: the teacher illustrates the behaviour she wants children to learn: for example, clapping in time to music or clapping out the rhythm of words or phrases. Imitation is a powerful means of teaching and learning.

● Prompting: the teacher encourages the child to respond, directing him towards the appropriate behaviour: 'Can you remember the next bit? It rhymes with…', 'Can you tell me what he's doing?'. If the response is not quite what the teacher is looking for, she can encourage a more appropriate one by asking questions, prompting, or modelling the behaviour again.

● Rewarding: the teacher rewards any appropriate response with praise and further encouragement. Praise will be more effective if it can emphasise what was good about the response: 'That was good. You were listening well', 'Well done, you remembered everything that happened'. Indiscriminate praise – praising anything and everything that children say or do – does not help them to learn.

Suitable activities for teaching the various skills are suggested in the Notes to the checklists. Children may need time to get used to some of these activities. Young children do not normally understand new things until they have experienced them several times, so it is important to repeat activities over at least a couple of weeks. If an activity is unfamiliar the teacher should first demonstrate it and explain why they are doing it; and at the end of the session she should highlight what they have been doing, why they have been doing it, and how well it all went.

Monitoring progress

Continuing assessment of children's progress is crucial for effective teaching, particularly with spoken language where it is so easy to overestimate children's abilities, or move them on before learning has been properly consolidated. Many – perhaps most – will already have the early behaviours in Checklist 1. But some may not, and the only way of knowing for sure which is which, and exactly which behaviours they do have, is by observing each child individually.

This need not be as onerous and time-consuming as it seems. The checklists provide a quick and simple way of recording individual progress. As each child exhibits a behaviour confidently, competently and consistently, it is ticked off on the checklist. This should not be on the basis of a single occasion. Each behaviour needs to be consistent – repeated and reliable – as well as confident and competent.

Staff may want to wait until the end of the week before reviewing all the children in their group and bringing the checklists up to date. The best test is whether children are showing a behaviour spontaneously, outside of small-group teaching. Behaviour should not be assessed on the basis of small-group work alone, and if there is any doubt about a particular behaviour it should not be credited. It is always better to underestimate children's abilities than overestimate them.

Staff also need to be sure that children are not just demonstrating that behaviour as a result of the week's teaching but have properly consolidated it. There can be considerable variation, from child to child and from skill to skill, in how long it takes to consolidate new learning. Most children consolidate new skills easily and naturally through normal classroom experience, but those who were slow to establish a skill in the first place are also likely to need longer to consolidate it. It can be useful to have some way of noting behaviours that are uncertain or inconsistent as well as those that seem to be firmly established, by, for example, using one tick for a skill that is hesitant or inconsistent and two ticks for one that is firmly established. Staff can then use this to gauge how long it is taking each child to consolidate a behaviour, and whether some forms of intervention are proving more effective than others.

Staff should also make a note of any behaviours that have proved difficult so they can go over them again later in the term, and should allow time for this in their long-term planning. They may need to come back to some of them several times, especially with children in the Delayed group. They should also allow a couple of weeks at the beginning of each term to check the previous term's learning; and then repeat teaching of any items that children seem to have forgotten. It is always more important that children consolidate basic skills than that they move on to more advanced ones.

KEY POINTS

- Each child is monitored separately using the checklists. As each child acquires a behaviour it is ticked off on the checklist.

- A behaviour or question form should only be credited when the child is using it confidently, competently and consistently. If there is any doubt about an item, it should not be credited.

- Staff need to ensure that each behaviour and question form has been properly consolidated, and should return later to any items that have proved difficult, to confirm that previous learning has been retained.

- It is always more important that children consolidate basic skills than that they move on to more advanced ones.

Moving on

The class normally keeps working on the same few question forms on a rolling basis, until everyone – or almost every one – has learnt them. As each question form is learnt, the teacher can include another one, and so on through the checklist. Each small group, similarly, works on the same few behaviours until everyone in that group has learnt them. Each group can work at its own pace but the pace of the group as a whole should always be geared to its slower members. It does not matter if some children are learning more quickly than others. It is always better to consolidate than push ahead too soon; all children will benefit from the extra practice; and if some of them can do some things comfortably, the others may be able to learn from them.

Early-years staff sometimes think they need to keep changing material or activities to retain children's interest and extend their experience, but, as every parent knows, young children like to repeat things over and over again: the same stories, the same songs, the same little phrases, the same little routines, day after day. Children under five will always benefit from repeating activities, particularly if they are having difficulty with the language that goes with them.

There may however come a time when a group just has to move on, because some children are becoming bored or frustrated, or are showing signs of stress or anxiety at the constant repetition. This might be a good time to reorganise teaching groups, or a group can come back to the same items later on, by which time the children having difficulty may be more ready for them. It is a good idea in any case to repeat any items that have proved difficult, as a way of reinforcing and consolidating everyone's learning as well as providing further support for those who need it.

It may also be convenient to keep the class more or less together. Intervention needs to be differentiated, to meet the needs of different children, but it also needs to be manageable.

With the question forms, in particular, it is much more convenient to have the whole class working on the same ones at the same time. So if one group has completed a particular skill, the teacher can mark time with them while she gives more attention to the other groups that are still working on it. Alternatively, she can let each group move on to the next skill as soon as they are ready, but this will mean that different groups are working on different skills, and that some groups may complete the checklist well before others.

Either way, it is much easier to manage if the class is working on only one checklist at a time. Staff should continue working on the same checklist until everyone – or almost everyone – has completed it. There may still be some children who are not ready to move on with the rest. If they are having particular difficulty with listening the most likely cause is an undiagnosed hearing problem (see Appendix 1). But there may also be some children who really need to keep working on the same few behaviours, but if they do they will only fall further and further behind. Depending on resources, it may be possible to keep them together for specialist small-group work, or provide some additional personal support.

Each checklist is expected to take about a term to complete but, allowing for the time needed for initial screening at the beginning of the year and for any preliminary work on Conversation Skills, it may not be possible to complete all three checklists within a school year. But what matters more than how far anyone gets is that everyone acquires the more basic skills before being expected to master more advanced ones.

It is, however, impossible to be precise about any of this. One size is not going to fit all, and staff will need to use their own experience and judgement in deciding when and how to move on from one behaviour, skill or checklist to the next.

KEY POINTS

- The class normally keeps working on the same question forms on a rolling basis, until everyone has learnt them.

- Each group normally keeps working on the same skill until everyone has learnt all the relevant behaviours, but it may sometimes be better to move on to another skill and come back to that one again later, or to reorganise the teaching groups.

- Each group can go at its own pace through the checklist but staff should wait until all groups have completed that checklist before proceeding to the next checklist.

- Special arrangements may have to be made for children or groups that are having particular difficulty.

- Each checklist is expected to take about a term to complete.

Links to literacy

Schools are under increasing pressure to introduce children to reading as soon as possible, yet many children starting school are simply not ready for reading or writing because they lack the necessary auditory skills. They need to be able to discriminate letter sounds in order to establish the link between sounds and letters and use that knowledge in reading, writing and spelling; they need to understand words and sentences easily in order to understand what they are reading; and they need to be able to follow and understand a story in order to produce a coherent text themselves. Helping children listen, understand and follow should be essential steps in a school's literacy strategy.

Children typically begin to acquire phonic skills from listening to and learning nursery rhymes and songs, playing with sound-making toys and instruments, and playing simple word-sound games like 'I spy'. Children who do not develop these skills may learn to read by recognising words as wholes, but will later have problems with spelling or reading new words because they cannot break the words down into separate sounds.

Children who have difficulty following spoken language will also have difficulty in understanding what they are reading. Some children learn the mechanics of reading in the sense that they can turn the written symbols into sounds, but have little idea of what they are reading. They can say the words but the underlying sense eludes them. This may not become obvious until the later primary years, when they have to use their reading to learn and find things out for themselves. To follow a description or explanation they have to understand more than the individual words and sentences; they have to understand how they fit together to make a whole. This is a skill children acquire originally from hearing and following stories.

> 'The inspection evidence…shows the importance of an emphasis on spoken language and the experience of being read to in many of the most effective schools. These help pupils to develop a vocabulary and an understanding of narrative or the structure of other texts, which they need to supplement phonic knowledge in order to read with full comprehension.'
>
> (Ofsted, 2005)

The extended listening that children need to develop at school also supports their writing. It helps add content to what they can write, familiarises them with longer descriptive accounts and different types of chronological and logical structure, and introduces the more formal types of language that are needed for most writing. The language and content of later 'free' writing is going to depend heavily on what they have heard or had read to them ('Once upon a time…'), more than on what they have read for themselves.

At the same time children should be developing other pre-literacy and literacy-support skills, including:

● Awareness, understanding and use of reading: By this age children ought to be thoroughly familiar with listening to stories and talking about them in some detail, showing some grasp of the narrative structure. They should also be enjoying looking at books on their own, turning the pages, following the pictures, and even 'reading' them to themselves or other children. Over the course of the year they should also be beginning to read – or at least recognise – some familiar words such as their own name or the signs around the classroom.

● Visual-motor skills: By now children ought to be thoroughly familiar with writing tools like pencils, crayons and felt pens, and be using them to draw, colour and scribble. Most will not be ready for copying or writing letter shapes, which call for much finer eye-hand co-ordination than is common at this age, but they should be able to trace and copy simple shapes or patterns, or continue 'tracks': for example, straight lines, curves, wavy lines or zig-zags.

● Awareness, understanding and use of writing: Staff should be talking to children about when and why we need to write things, and the different ways we can do this. Helping them to 'write' their own signs, labels, lists, greetings in cards or notes to each other or their parents helps introduce the idea of different types of writing for different purposes, as well as introducing them to the mechanics of writing.

Child's name	Band 1	Can follow simple instructions	Can answer simple questions	Will join in simple nursery rhymes	Band 2	Can clap or march in time to music	Learns new nursery rhymes easily	Can link several different sounds to the objects or animals that make them	Competent	Developing	Delayed
_____											
_____											
_____											
_____											
_____											
_____											
_____											
_____											
_____											
_____											
_____											
_____											
_____											
_____											
_____											
_____											
_____											
_____											

- Children who lack any of the behaviours in Band 1 are identified as *Delayed*, even if they have some of the behaviours in Band 2.

- Children who have all the behaviours in Band 1 but lack any of the behaviours in Band 2 are identified as *Developing*.

- Children who have all the behaviours in both Bands are identified as *Competent*.

Teaching Speaking and Listening © Ann Locke (Bloomsbury Publishing plc, 2013)

Teaching Speaking and Listening © Ann Locke (Bloomsbury Publishing plc, 2013)

Listening Skills, *Checklist 1*   Understanding instructions and questions

One Step at a Time

Child's name

Following instructions

												Can follow a simple instruction
												Can follow an instruction to fetch two separate objects
												Can follow an instruction to fetch three objects
												Can follow a sequence of simple instructions
												Can follow a sequence of complex instructions

Early question forms

												Understands *What's that?*
												Understands *Where is …?*
												Understands *Who is …?*
												Understands *What is/are ….. doing?*
												Understands *Who can …?*

Later question forms

												Understands *What's that for?*
												Understands *When?*
												Understands *Why?*
												Understands *How?*

Child's name													

Hearing rhythms and rhymes

												Can do the correct actions in action songs
												Can march or clap in time to unfamiliar music
												Learns new nursery rhymes easily
												Can complete the missing rhymes in familiar nursery rhymes

Identifying sounds

												Knows several pretend sounds that go with different animals or objects
												Can identify an object or musical instrument by the sound it makes, out of two
												Can identify an object or musical instrument by the sound it makes, out of three
												Can copy a sequence of two sounds, using instruments or objects
												Can copy a sequence of three sounds, using instruments or objects

Discriminating sounds in words

												Can clap out the rhythm of a word or phrase
												Given a word, can repeat the initial sound
												Given a sound, can find a word that begins with it
												Can play 'I Spy'
												Given a word, can find a rhyme
												Given a word, can repeat the final sound

Using word memory

												Can recite several rhymes or poems by heart
												Can play memory games, remembering at least three items
												Can play memory games, remembering at least five items

Teaching Speaking and Listening © Ann Locke (Bloomsbury Publishing plc, 2013)

Child's name

Understanding pictures

| | Can name people and objects in picture scenes |
| | Can say what is happening in picture scenes |

Understanding stories

	Can name characters or objects in a story, using the pictures
	Can say what is happening in a story, using the pictures
	Can name characters or objects in a story without using the pictures
	Can say what is happening in a story without using the pictures
	Can say what happens next in a familiar story, using the pictures
	Can say what happens next in a familiar story without using the pictures

Understanding time

	Can comment on or answer questions about current events
	Can comment on or answer questions about past events
	Understands *What will happen next?*
	Understands *What will happen if…?*

Understanding implicit meanings

	Can identify objects, animals etc. from a verbal description
	Can link picture scenes to personal experience
	Can link events in a story to personal experience
	Can offer an explanation of what is going on in a picture scene
	Can offer an explanation of what is going on in a story

Vocabulary wordlist

Listening skills

Quality	Colour	Texture	Sound	Shape	Size	Quantity	Number	Space	Time	Movement	Feelings and emotion
different	brown	rough	high	cross	bigger	a few	both	above	always	along	afraid
light	dark	shiny	loudly	pattern	deep	each	half	across	before	around	angry
old	orange	smooth	low	shape	fat	enough	next	against	early	forwards	bad
plain	pink		quietly	star	large	every	penny	below	late	quickly	careful
same	white		silent		longest	less	pound	beside	later	sideways	cross
striped			soft		short	most	second	between	never	slowly	dangerous
					smaller	much	third	bottom	night-time	towards	friendly
					thin	nearly	twice	close (to)	sometimes		helpful
						none		facing	summer		lovely
						plenty		far	winter		pleased
						very		high			safe
						whole		low			tired
								middle			uncomfortable
								(a) space			unkind
								together			
								top			

Teaching Speaking and Listening © Ann Locke (Bloomsbury Publishing plc, 2013)

NOTES ON CHECKLIST 1

Understanding instructions and questions

This checklist deals with children's understanding of simple classroom language. Most children at this age will have these skills already, but staff need to ensure that all children have them.

Understanding can be difficult to assess, especially in whole-class activities. If children do not respond it is easy to assume that they have not been paying attention, and their failure to understand gets misdiagnosed as a failure to attend. If they have poor auditory memories or find it difficult to keep up with rapid spoken language they may develop coping strategies like using visual clues or their knowledge of classroom routines: they may not be following what is said, merely following other children. Even the fact that they use a word or expression does not necessarily mean they understand it. Some children learn to say the appropriate thing without really understanding what they are saying. Understanding is best assessed in the to-and-fro of one-to-one conversation, where adults can tell from children's responses how much they really understand.

Following instructions

The ability to follow instructions is not just an essential classroom skill, it also helps develop children's memories, including their auditory memory. Teaching can begin with simple instructions like 'Bring me that book'; then move to complex instructions for familiar routines like 'Put on your coat and gloves, and go and stand by the door'; then to complex unfamiliar instructions like 'Go and get a red ball and a blue ball from the basket, keep one and give the other one to your friend'. Break-time, playground games, PE and music sessions all provide good opportunities for teaching instructions and directions, but it is important to avoid routines that are very familiar, because children may already know what to do, without even listening to the instruction.

Children who have difficulty following directions may have poor auditory attention or poor memory for speech. They can be helped by starting with simple instructions like 'Find something blue' with sets of pictures, objects or shapes, and building up to more complex instructions like 'Point to something in the picture and find something just like it on the table'. These activities can be fun for children, are easily managed in small-group sessions, and help them remember sequences of actions. It is important, however, to proceed slowly and not move to complex instructions too quickly. It can help if teachers draw up a list of instructions in order of difficulty, and work through them one at a time, introducing the next instruction only when the children are ready.

For further suggestions for appropriate small-group activities see Chapter 2 of the Activities Handbook in *Teaching Talking* (Locke and Beech, 2005).

Early question forms

Question form teaching can run in parallel with other skills teaching. It can be introduced as soon as children are ready – they do not need to complete Following instructions first – and can also continue while they move on to the second checklist. It can easily take more than a term to cover all nine early and late question forms with all children.

Note that the emphasis at this stage is on whether the child understands a particular type of question, not whether he can ask it. Asking questions is covered in the next level of the programme. The two will often happen together in circle-time or small-group work, but the test here is just whether children can answer the question appropriately, not whether they can use it themselves to obtain information.

The best way to teach question forms is to feature them one at a time as 'the question of the week' or 'this week's special question'. The teacher can start the week by discussing this question with her class: why we need it, how we use it, and what it can help us to find out. She should then highlight that question wherever possible and incorporate it into classroom teaching at least once a day over the rest of the week, during story-time, circle-time, talk-time or any other suitable activity, as well as in small-group work, especially with children who are finding questions difficult. She should also display the current question in a prominent position in the classroom where she and the children can easily refer to it.

This 'question of the week' can be changed week by week if most children are learning it, but the class should also come back to the same question forms more than once to consolidate learning, as well as for the sake of any children who are learning more slowly. It does no harm for other children to repeat the same questions in whole-class work, but staff may also need to provide more targeted intervention for some children in small-group work.

A useful aid for teaching questions at a small-group, larger group or whole-class level is a 'Questions table' with a variety of interesting and intriguing objects or pictures which staff and children can use for asking each other the current question of the week. As they become familiar with the exercise, children can also use the table to work in pairs or without adult support. The items displayed will probably need to alter as the question changes, and children can be encouraged to bring their own items to include on the table, so they can ask other children about them.

Later question forms

Both Earlier and Later question forms are taught on a rolling basis, one question at a time, with class returning to some forms again and again until all (or almost all) children have learnt them. The Later question forms, however, are more difficult, and should be kept separate: that is, the class should not start working on them until they have learnt all the earlier forms. They are also more difficult to introduce and illustrate. Familiar items like a ball of string, a shopping bag, rubber bands or sticky tape can be used to ask 'What's this for?', 'When do we use it?' or 'Why do we need it?'; sequences of pictures that illustrate making a drink or peeling an apple can be used to explain 'How?' or 'Why?' questions; and so on.

NOTES ON CHECKLIST 2

Hearing sounds and word patterns

This checklist develops children's discrimination of sound and word patterns in preparation for the use of phonics in teaching reading. It is not itself a phonics programme but a way of ensuring that all children have the abilities they need for using phonics. The importance of phonics in teaching reading is widely recognised but the underlying abilities are not so well understood.

This checklist is, in effect, a pre-phonics programme and can be used as part of a phonics teaching programme. Many of the activities and some of the skills will be the same. Some of the activities will in any case be familiar in every early-years classroom, and part of normal classwork throughout the year. In particular, songs and nursery rhymes should be included from early in Term 1 so children are thoroughly familiar with them before they start working on them specifically in this part of the programme. For further suggestions for appropriate small group activities see Chapters 2 and 9 of the Activities Handbook in *Teaching Talking* (Locke and Beech, 2005).

Hearing rhythms and rhymes

Simple speech-action games like 'Miss Polly had a dolly' or 'This is the church and this is the steeple' encourage children to listen to the sound of words. Clapping, moving or marching in time to music help them to hear the rhythm of words and syllables. Nursery rhymes encourage children to enjoy the sound of words and recognise different sound patterns, and also develop their auditory memory. By this stage they should know several nursery rhymes and songs, and be learning new ones fairly easily. Getting them to complete familiar rhymes – 'Hey diddle diddle, the cat and the…?', 'Little Jack Horner sat in the …?' – is a way of tuning them into word sound-patterns, and introduces them to the idea of words that rhyme or 'sound the same'.

Nursery rhymes can be taught in small-group work, in larger groups, or as a whole-class activity. New rhymes can be introduced in a rolling programme, one by one, with no more than three rhymes being learnt at any one time. Each rhyme should be repeated every day for at least three weeks.

Identifying sounds

Before children can learn to recognise and identify the sounds in words they need to be able to recognise natural sounds, and identify things around them by the sound they make. This helps to develop auditory discrimination and auditory memory.

Most children will be able to identify simple pretend sounds like *bow-wow*, *tick-tock* or *brrmm-brrmm*, though some may need to be taught them. But they should also be introduced to natural sounds – clocks, cars, birds etc. – in the classroom and outside ('What do you think is making that noise?'). If the teacher makes a tape-recording of familiar sounds, she can play it back and see if children can identify the sounds without having the thing itself as a clue.

Musical instruments, or collections of tins or boxes containing beans, buttons, wooden blocks or nails so they each make a different noise, can be used to teach children to identify sequences of sounds, and then repeat them. At first they can watch as the teacher makes the sounds, but eventually they should be able to identify the sounds without seeing what she is doing.

Discriminating sounds in words

Auditory discrimination – the ability to separate the sounds that go to make up words – is essential for phonics work, and eventually for reading, writing and spelling. Children can be helped to separate syllables and word or letter sounds by clapping out the rhythms of familiar words and phrases: for example, *cro-co-dile*, *salt-and-pep-per*.

Most children of this age should be able to identify and repeat the initial sound in a word, though the target sound may need to be emphasised at first: *mmm-mouse*, *sss-sand*. Finding a word that begins with a given sound is more difficult because they have to think of a word while remembering the sound. Playing 'I spy' using pictures or objects is a useful way of reinforcing and developing these skills. At first the teacher leads, with the children having to find a word that begins with that sound. Then the children can take it in turns to lead. They will find this more difficult, because they have to find an object, remember its name, and isolate the initial sound – all without giving it away!

Most children will also find it difficult to identify the final sounds in words: *run-n*, *hill-l*. A useful first step is being able to recognise single-syllable rhymes. At first the teacher may have to give several rhyming words and help them to find another: *hat – mat – pat – cat*; *red – head – said – bed*. But as they grow familiar with the activity, they should be able to find rhymes for a single word themselves: *far – car*; *now – cow*. Rhyming puzzles and rhyming cards (pictures of things with rhyming names) can be helpful here. Finding a word that ends with a given sound is too difficult for most children at this stage.

Using word memory

Reciting nursery rhymes by heart rather than repeating them in a group is an important test of children's auditory memory. Memory games like 'I went shopping and I bought a...' or 'I went on the bus and I saw a...' help to develop children's memory in general – essential for all learning – as well as their memories for words and meanings.

Memory games can be introduced in circle-time or small-group sessions. If some children find these games difficult, try simpler games like 'Copy me' or 'What did I forget?' In 'Copy me' the teacher first gets each child to repeat after her a simple list of words like hands – *feet – toes* or *bus – car – truck*, then phrases like *very silly boys*, *soon be bedtime* or *two tiny toes*, and then sentences like 'We are going to the shop to buy some bread' or 'We had bread and jam for our tea'. In 'What did I forget?' the teacher puts several objects on a table, names them all except one, and the child has to say which one was left out.

NOTES ON CHECKLIST 3

Understanding meaning

This checklist deals with children's understanding of narrative, time and implicit meaning. It will also help them develop the extended listening that they need in school and is very different from the conversational listening they will be used to at home.

Choice of material is more than usually important. Teachers will need to find story books or other texts that are suitable for teaching understanding, and then work out a series of questions that explore first the literal meaning, then the implicit meanings. These books and questions should be graded by difficulty, and introduced one by one. It will also help to have a table with a set of pictures, toys or other objects illustrating or relevant to the current story, as well as the book itself, to encourage children to talk about the story, and 'read' it themselves or to other children.

Understanding pictures

Pictures are the best place to start because they are easier to understand than texts. They need to be scenes, which have something happening in them, and more than one person or item, not just a single object. Children should first be asked to identify people or things in the picture ('What's that?', 'Who do you think that lady is?'), then to describe what is going on ('What is the boy doing?'). As they progress the pictures can become more complex and detailed. Children need to be able to handle moderately complex pictures before moving to understanding stories.

Understanding stories

Telling children stories is a key way in which we teach them about people and how they behave. It is also a valuable way of showing them the pleasures of reading. But first they need to be able to follow the story.

The teacher should start by using the pictures to ask questions about the characters while she is telling the story. She reads a bit, then checks understanding by asking 'Who's this?', 'What has he got?', and so on. Then she can ask questions without using the pictures as a clue: 'Who knocked at the door?', 'Who climbed up the beanstalk?' Questions that come at the end of a story will be more difficult for children to answer because they have to remember what happened. Teachers can try this – beginning with the same questions they asked earlier – but should not expect all children to respond, especially at first. The next step is to see whether they can say what is happening in the story, first using the pictures, then without them. Finally, the teacher should check their understanding of the sequence of events by telling part of the story and asking 'What happens now?' or 'What happened next?'.

Children who have difficulty holding a narrative in their head, or seem not to have any idea of a narrative, can be helped by using felts or magnetic boards to build up a story step by step, or picture cards that can be laid out in sequence to tell a story. It can also be very effective to use a computer or a camera to create your own sequences of pictures of familiar domestic activities or classroom routines, especially if the pictures can include the children themselves. At this stage children are not expected to put the pictures in sequence or tell the story themselves. They just need to be able to follow a sequence.

Understanding time

At first children use language in relation to present events and the things that they can currently see and hear. It takes time for them to develop and understand language that refers to the past, and especially the future. This goes hand in hand with the development of verb tenses.

Children's understanding of present, past and future is developed and assessed through the sort of questioning that occurs in all classroom work. A good way of promoting their understanding of time is to have a large pictorial timetable showing all the days of the week including the weekend, and use it every day to talk about what has happened or will happen. This will model and encourage the use of verb tenses and other time vocabulary as well as helping children to organise and plan their work and other activities.

Understanding *What will happen next?* or *What will happen if....?* is more complex than understanding tenses but is needed for explanation and prediction, and for more sophisticated writing. At first these questions should be about familiar activities in the classroom or outside, but they can later include pictures and stories.

Understanding implicit meaning

Children need to understand the meanings behind pictures and stories, including why the characters behave as they do: 'Some children were going out to play. Their mother asked them to put their coats and boots on first. Why do you think she said that?'

Children first need to be able to identify people, animals and objects from just a description, without using pictures. Then they should be able to explain what is going on first in a picture, then in a story. For example, shown a picture of a crying boy with blood on his knee, they need to know not just what he is doing (surface meaning) but why (implicit meaning). You may be surprised how difficult some children find this! Stories call for more complex explanations: 'Why did the dog run away?', 'Why did the man chase him?'.

One effective way of helping children understand the wider meaning of pictures and stories is by relating them to personal experience. At first the questions can be factual: 'Have you got a pet?', 'Is your dog sometimes naughty?', 'What do you do then?'. Then you can begin to explore feelings and motivations: 'Has that ever happened to you?', 'Did you cry?', 'What did your mummy do?', 'Why did she do that?'.

Chapter 10 Narrative Skills

Narrative Skills is a programme for developing children's ability to talk and think about the present, past and future, in preparation for writing and other demands of the early school curriculum. It is intended for children aged five to seven who have previously done Listening Skills. If a significant number of children have not had this experience it is recommended that the whole class does some Listening Skills work before commencing Narrative Skills. Partly to allow for this, Narrative Skills is expected to extend across two years, but will still benefit all children where it can only be used for a single year.

This level of the programme aims to develop children's ability to talk independently and extensively, without the support provided by conversation, and at greater length. As children begin to move into the formal curriculum they need to develop more extended forms of talking, such as describing things and events, reporting activities, recounting experiences, retelling stories, explaining how something was made, or predicting the outcomes of actions or experiments. Although quite young children are able to talk about the immediate past, children as old as five or six can find it difficult to remember or describe a series of events in sequence, and it may take some of them all their primary years to establish consistency in the use of verb tenses or a proper grasp of personal pronouns. These skills need to be developed systematically, but while children get lots of practice in extended listening at school, they get much less practice in extended talking. They may be sitting listening for much of the day but asked to 'give their news' barely once a week.

Narrative promotes children's thinking skills by helping them develop coherent sequences of ideas. It gets them to clarify their thoughts by talking them over, thinking them through out loud. It develops their understanding of time, of the past and future as well as the present. It trains them in asking questions and using different verb forms. It introduces ideas of possibility and probability, of what *would* happen or *could* happen or *should* happen. These skills are important for history, science and technology as well as literacy.

They are especially important for writing. To write even a simple account, children have to: think of something to write about, put the events in the right order, mention key facts and exclude irrelevant detail, and provide a beginning and an ending. There is then the added difficulty of having to turn all this into marks on paper, or perhaps a computer screen. Since talking is easier than writing they can develop these skills through extended talk, such as describing a picture, recalling an outing, retelling a story, anticipating what is going to happen or explaining how to do something.

Speech propels writing forward. Pupils do not improve writing solely by doing more of it; good quality writing benefits from focused discussion that gives pupils a chance to talk through ideas before writing.

(Ofsted, 2005)

Narrative Skills is primarily intended for children aged five to seven who have already done Listening Skills. In a class where a significant number of children have not had this experience, or did not complete the previous level, it is recommended that they all have some practice with listening skills first, before beginning Narrative Skills. How much work they will need on Conversation Skills will depend on their age, ability and confidence but they should at least work through Checklist 3, which features skills that are needed for narrative work. Younger children, aged five to six, should start with the Checklist 2, because it features pre-phonics skills that are important for early reading.

Children who have completed Narrative Skills will be more confident in expressing themselves. They will be able to talk independently and at length about events, situations and objects, and able to clarify their thoughts by talking them through or asking questions. They will be able to describe and predict and understand the differences between past, present and future, or between what is actual and what is possible. They will have more confidence in writing, because they will know what to write and how to write it.

Initial screening

The initial screen helps teachers:

- 'tune-in' to the relevant skills at this level of the programme
- identify children's current development of these skills
- determine the amount of support they are likely to need.

The first of these may be the most important. For Narrative Skills teachers need to be aware of children's ability to use language for purposes other than conversation: questioning, describing, recounting, reporting, predicting, suggesting, obtaining and using information. They need to be aware of children's ability to put separate pieces of information together into a coherent structure: for example, mention the right things in the right order. They need to be aware of the structure of what children are saying: for example, their use of pronouns, tenses and time or sequence markers.

They also need to be aware of the differences in these skills between children, so they can provide the targeted support that is needed. Which children ask questions as well as answering them? Different types of question? Which children talk fluently in sentences? More than one sentence at a time? Which children can give a coherent account of something?

All this can be more difficult than it might seem. Teachers may not be used to discriminating these behaviours, or identifying them in individual children. These are the skills they need to develop, and the screening process can help them do it.

The initial screen is a quick and simple measure of current development, not a formal assessment. It identifies children as:

- Competent: they seem to be acquiring these skills without too much difficulty and are not expected to need special attention.

- Developing: they seem to be slower in acquiring these skills and are likely to need some support and attention.

- Delayed: they seem to be having difficulty in acquiring these skills and are likely to need more intensive support and attention.

These groupings are intended to be flexible and are likely to change in the course of a term or year.

Screening should not be carried out until children have settled into their new class and become used to their new environment. This may take several weeks, especially if children have just started school. But it does give the class teacher time to observe children informally in a variety of situations, focusing on the skills to be assessed.

The screen can then be completed, with a colleague if possible. Children's behaviour can still be variable and a second opinion is always useful. It is also easy to take some of these behaviours for granted, or underestimate the skills of quiet children and overestimate the skills of more talkative ones.

Each child needs to be considered separately. Teachers are often surprised to discover that while it seems 'the whole class' can do something, there are actually huge variations in what individual children contribute and their level of detail or accuracy, with some of them barely understanding what the task is.

It is also important to consider each behaviour separately. A behaviour should only be credited if a child is using it confidently, competently and consistently. If there is any doubt or disagreement, the behaviour should not be credited. It is always better to underestimate abilities than overestimate them.

The initial screen has two bands, and children are assessed band by band. That is, if they do not have all the behaviours in Band 1, they do not need to be assessed on Band 2.

- Children who lack any of the behaviours in Band 1 are identified as Delayed, even if they have some of the behaviours in Band 2.

- Children who have all the behaviours in Band 1 but lack any of the behaviours in Band 2 are identified as Developing.

- Children who have all the behaviours in both bands are identified as Competent.

The Delayed group may include some children with special educational needs but should not be thought of as a special needs group. Children can be delayed for all sorts of reasons, including lack of confidence, lack of experience, or lack of familiarity with the English language; and some children with special needs may have perfectly adequate language skills, or show uneven patterns of development. Children with special needs may need extra support but should be included in the *One Step* programme in the same way as any other child. For further guidance see Appendix 1.

Children whose listening skills seem delayed or whose speech is unclear or jumbled may have an undiagnosed hearing problem or a specific language difficulty. Again, see Appendix 1.

KEY POINTS

- While children are settling into their new class, teachers can be observing them informally in a variety of situations, focusing on the behaviours to be assessed.

- Working with a colleague if possible, the class teacher completes the initial screen for each child separately.

- A behaviour should be credited only if a child is using it competently, confidently and consistently. If there is any doubt or disagreement, the behaviour should not be credited.

- The screen has two bands, and children are assessed band by band. If they do not have all the behaviours in Band 1, they do not need to be assessed on Band 2.

- Children who lack any of the behaviours in Band 1 are identified as Delayed, even if they have some of the behaviours in Band 2.

- Children who have all the behaviours in Band 1 but lack some of the behaviours in Band 2 are identified as Developing.

- Children who have all the behaviours in both bands are identified as Competent.

Skills checklists

Narrative Skills uses three skills checklists to focus and guide classroom intervention and monitor individual progress:

- Talking about the present
- Talking about the past
- Talking about the future.

Each checklist consists of Question forms (a question form is a general type of question like 'What is …? or 'Who can …?'), Describing the present, past or future, and Sequencing. Each of these is divided in turn into a number of separate items or behaviours. Describing the Present, for example, includes being able to name people or things, being able to describe what people are wearing, and being able to talk about a familiar DVD or TV programme. It will be convenient to refer to each group of items as a skill and the separate items, including the question forms, as behaviours.

These skills, behaviours and question forms are listed in rough developmental order as a guide to intervention. Different children will of course show different patterns of development, and some of them – especially those identified as Competent – will have some or all of the behaviours already or be able to establish them almost immediately. But others may need to learn them one by one.

Children normally work through each checklist in sequence but at different speeds and with varying degrees of support, usually one skill at a time. With Narrative Skills, however, the question forms can run in parallel with the other skills. In the first checklist, for example, the class can start with Question forms and then add Describing the present, so they are doing both together; but they should complete Describing the present before starting on Sequencing.

Children will also often be working on more than one behaviour or question form at a time. Items that go together get learnt together; in working on one, the teacher will usually have been introducing another; and this provides an easy transition from one item to the next. Some children will show some or all of the relevant behaviours already, or be able to establish them almost immediately. Others may need to learn them slowly, one by one.

Each behaviour and question form is, however, assessed separately. Teachers need to be confident that each child has established them, and the only way to be sure of that is to work through the checklists systematically, ticking them off one by one.

KEY POINTS

- Each checklist includes Question forms, Describing and Sequencing, divided into separate behaviours or question forms.

- Skills and behaviours are listed in rough developmental order as a guide to intervention.

- Children normally work through each checklist in sequence. Question forms are introduced first. Describing can then be introduced to run in parallel, followed by Sequencing, but not all three at the same time.

- Teaching of different behaviours and question forms will usually overlap.

- Every child and every item needs to be assessed and monitored separately

---

Classroom intervention

Narrative skills are taught through a mixture of whole-class and small-group or partner work, supported by informal interaction with individual children. The checklists set specific objectives for all children on a rolling basis, while the initial screens help determine the amount of support needed for each child. Question forms are most easily introduced with the class as a whole but can be practised and consolidated in small-group and/or partner work. Describing and Sequencing both need small-group or partner work using appropriate materials. Detailed advice on intervention for specific skills and behaviours is given in the Notes to each checklist.

Whole-class work

Whole-class work is used to introduce new activities, teach question forms, reinforce and consolidate learning across the curriculum.

Suitable activities for teaching the various skills are suggested in the Notes to the checklists. With Describing and Sequencing the teacher may need to start by explaining any new activities or materials; sequencing cards, in particular, can take some getting used to. As well as demonstrating an activity herself, she can get some of the children to try it too, though this may be more effective if done in small groups first, especially for children who are likely to find it difficult.

The best way to teach the question forms is to feature them one at a time as 'the question of the week' or 'this week's special question'. The teacher can start the week by discussing this question with her class, explaining how we use it, why we need it, and what it helps us to find out. Even better, she can ask the class to explain it and give examples. She should then try to incorporate that question into classroom teaching at least once a day over the rest of the week, during story-time, circle-time, talk-time or any other suitable activity, and in small-group and partner work. In circle-time, for example, the teacher can put a pile of objects or a set of pictures in the middle of the circle, and children can take turns, going round the circle, to ask each other the question of the week. She should also display the current question in a prominent position in the classroom where she and the children can easily refer to it.

This 'question of the week' can be changed week by week if most children are learning it but the class should also come back to the same question forms more than once, to consolidate learning, as well as for the sake of any children who are learning more slowly. It does no harm for other children to repeat question forms in whole-class work, but the teacher may also need to provide more targeted intervention for some children in group and partner work.

As well as this specific focus on current skills at least once a day, almost any classroom activity can be used to support and reinforce current learning, at any time, several times a day. This will gives all children valuable experience of skills being used in different situations and contexts, with different adults, and by different children. But the teacher also needs to be aware of any children who are finding particular behaviours or question forms difficult, and be sure that they are actually following and participating, rather than letting it all go over their heads.

Small-group work

Small-group work is used to teach describing and sequencing skills, and to reinforce and consolidate learning, especially with younger children (five to six years old) who may not be not ready for partner work. Each child can be assigned to a teaching group on the basis of the initial screen, possibly including, where appropriate, some mixed-ability groupings: Delayed with Developing or Developing with Competent, but not Delayed with Competent, because the Competent children are likely to dominate when it is the Delayed children who need the practice.

These groups need to be kept small. 'Group work' can sometimes mean as many as ten or 12 children; for language work it should ideally be no more than six. Many children will find it difficult to understand or concentrate in a larger group. In a smaller group they can follow and join in, the teacher can relate to each child in turn, and other children in the group can learn from the exchange.

Groups also need to be kept small so staff can assess each child individually. With a larger group it is easy to think that everyone can do something when in fact some children are barely participating, if they are participating at all. Video evidence has shown, for example, that while the teacher felt that the children never stopped talking, some actually said very little or even showed much awareness of what was going on.

Each small-group teaching session should last 15 to 20 minutes. Children identified as Delayed should ideally receive two or three sessions a week, working specifically on their narrative skills. Children identified as Developing should receive one or two sessions a week if possible. Children identified as Competent will probably need at most one session a week.

- Small-group work is used to teach describing and sequencing skills, and to reinforce and consolidate learning, especially with younger children who may not be ready for partner work.

- Children are assigned to teaching groups of six to eight children on the basis of the initial screen. Children identified as Delayed should receive two or three small-group sessions a week if possible.

- Each teaching session should be 15 to 20 minutes long.

Partner work

Partner work is a very useful addition at this level but is recommended for older children who are experienced in working in small groups. Children aged five to six will be more comfortable working in small groups at first.

It is, moreover, a valuable teaching tool in its own right. It takes pressure off teachers by allowing children to work on their own but is easier to manage than independent group work. It boosts the confidence and general language skills of anxious or less able children. It can provide the extra practice, consolidation and generalisation that children need but is difficult to achieve in schools. It can even ensure that all children get to practise their narrative skills each and every day. It enables children to learn from and support each other as well as learning from their teacher, something our education system does not encourage often enough. And children enjoy it.

In fact, partner work has proved so successful that teachers have found that it soon becomes an integral part of everyday classroom practice. It can be used to deliver almost any part of the curriculum or consolidate almost any piece of whole-class work: 'Now turn to your talking partner and…'. Instead of asking her class a question, which only one child can answer, the teacher can get her talking partners to ask each other, and then discuss some sample answers with the whole class.

Partner work may seem daunting and potentially disruptive at first but teachers should not be afraid to 'let go'. There tend to be two main concerns: that it will be too noisy, and that children will not stay on topic. Experience does not support either concern: 'It's amazing what children can do when you put them to it!'. Noise should not be a problem if, for example, children are told to use their 'small' voice for partner work and their 'big' voice in whole-class lessons; and they will usually remain on topic provided the task is clear and appropriate, within their capabilities, and not allowed to go on for too long.

Children need to be thoroughly used to partner work in general before it is used to teach narrative skills. The teacher should first explain to her class what partner work is, how it works, and what the rules are: listening to each other, not talking for too long, taking turns, etc. She can then demonstrate what she means using different children as a partner, and get her class to practise it for themselves, at first with simple, familiar tasks. She will need to repeat this several times over days or weeks, introducing different and gradually less familiar tasks, to get her class thoroughly familiar with the procedure.

Each exercise also has to be introduced first at a whole-class level. In particular, the various skills and behaviours from the checklists need to be explained and demonstrated in whole-class work before being practised in partner work. This too may need to be repeated over several days until children are thoroughly familiar both with the general procedure and with what they need to be doing on this occasion. They are much more likely to work productively together and demonstrate the relevant behaviours or question forms if they know exactly what is expected of them and what they should be expecting from each other.

The teacher should obviously try to pair children who are compatible and likely to support each other. Partner work also seems to work better if less able or more anxious children are paired with stronger or more confident children: Competent with Developing, or Developing with Delayed – but perhaps not Competent with Delayed. The teacher should also keep a close eye on any children identified as Delayed and sometimes act as their partner.

It may also be better, both pedagogically and socially, for children to have different partners at different times or for different lessons. As they become more experienced in this way of working, they can sometimes be allowed to choose their own partners, though the teacher may need to make sure that they do not always choose the same one or that the same children are not always left over.

Each separate exercise should last only a few minutes, especially at first. The teacher can then, if she wishes, set another exercise. At the end of the session she should thank her class for working well together, and highlight any good points such as not making too much noise. A good way of providing whole-class feedback is to have a 'hot seat': one child sits in the hot seat and tells the rest of the class what he and his partner have been doing.

KEY POINTS

● Older children can be paired for partner work. Using partner work it should be possible for children to practise narrative skills almost every day.

● Children need to be thoroughly used to partner work in general before it is used to teach narrative skills.

● The teacher should introduce, explain and demonstrate each exercise, and the specific behaviours she is targeting, so children know what is expected of them.

Informal interaction

There are also many spare moments in the day that staff can use to engage with children individually. The daily routines of entering and leaving the classroom, waiting in line, preparation and tidying up, snack and meal times, all provide good opportunities for practising question forms with individual children, and talking about what they are doing, have done or will be doing. Some of the behaviours, especially under Sequencing, need specific materials or activities, but others – like talking about a TV programme – can be practised at any time.

This is, moreover, where everyone can help. Everyone – not just teachers and classroom assistants but lunchtime supervisors, playground assistants and site staff – has a role to play in making time to talk with individual children. It should be part of every school activity – daily routines, lessons, outings and visits – that adults talk with children about them, individually and together, before it has begun, while it is happening, and when it is finished. And not just staff: parents, grandparents and visitors (especially inspectors) too.

A list of items currently being worked on should be displayed prominently in the classroom and given to parents, so everyone can see and refer to it and use it to guide their interaction with individual children.

KEY POINTS

- **A list of items currently being worked on should be displayed prominently, and given to parents, so everyone can use it to guide their interaction with individual children.**

- **All staff and other adults should be encouraged to use every available opportunity to practise these skills with children individually.**

Vocabulary work

Children's development of vocabulary is crucial for their progress through school but vocabulary work is mostly an optional element in *One Step at a Time*, for reasons given in Chapter 12. For teachers who want to include systematic vocabulary work, Narrative Skills provides a list of 100 essential words selected from the vocabulary of property and relations and the vocabulary of feelings and emotion as discussed in Chapter 2. This list is intended to be supplemented with essential topic vocabulary as explained in Chapter 12.

Lesson planning

Teachers usually want to decide in advance what they are going to teach, when they are going to teach it and how they are going to teach it, so they can prepare lessons, select activities, gather resources, inform other staff, advise parents, and so on. But planning also needs to be flexible because some skills may take longer to learn than expected, and sometimes very much longer.

Lesson planning includes setting objectives, selecting topics or activities, preparing materials, and allocating times. The skills checklists provide teaching and learning objectives for all children. Suggestions for appropriate activities are given in the Notes to each checklist. The materials will need to include a collection of picture scenes, varying in detail and familiarity, and several sets of sequencing cards. A good place to start for describing and sequencing are sets of photos taken of – or even by – the children themselves, during familiar routines at school or at home.

A useful aid for teaching questions at a small-group, larger group or whole-class level is a 'Questions table' with a variety of interesting and intriguing objects or pictures which staff and children can use to ask each other the current question of the week. As they become familiar with the exercise, children can also use the table to work in pairs on their own. The items displayed will probably need to alter as the question changes, and children can be encouraged to bring their own items to include on the table, so they can ask other children about them.

As well as allocating specific times for small-group or other language work, staff should also identify some activities every day where current learning can be consolidated. Similarly, longer-term planning should include some weeks when teaching groups can go back and repeat any work they have found difficult. This is particularly important for children identified as Delayed, to ensure that all learning has been properly consolidated.

Teaching method

The most effective teaching techniques are those that parents use to teach their children, usually without realising they are doing it (see Chapter 3):

- Highlighting: the teacher draws attention to the relevant behaviour by discussing it, explaining its importance, or explaining when or why we do it: for example, she can discuss why we like stories, why we tell them, and how we go about telling them. She can do this by asking questions – 'What do we do first?, 'What happens then?' – and discussing the children's responses, then summarising and highlighting the key points: 'So when we tell a story we have to say who the people are, and then what happened to them, bit by bit, in the right order'.

- Modelling: the teacher illustrates the behaviour she wants children to learn: for example, she describes a familiar TV programme, or how she made something, then encourages the children to do the same. Imitation is a powerful means of teaching and learning.

- Prompting: the teacher encourages the child to respond, directing him towards the appropriate behaviour: 'What happens next?', 'What do you think that boy is going to do?' 'Can you think of another ending?'. If a response is not quite what the adult is looking for, she can encourage a more appropriate one by asking questions, prompting or modelling the behaviour again.

- Rewarding: the teacher rewards any appropriate response with praise and further encouragement. Praise will be more effective if it can emphasise what was good about the response: 'Well done, Mary. You told Asif lots about your picture'; 'Good thinking, William! That would make a good ending'. Indiscriminate praise – praising anything and everything that children say or do – does not help them to learn.

Suitable activities for teaching the various skills are suggested in the Notes to each checklist. Children may need time to get used to some of them. They may not understand an activity until they have practised it several times, so it is important to repeat unfamiliar activities over at least a couple of weeks.

Monitoring progress

Continuing assessment of children's progress is crucial for effective teaching, particularly with spoken language where it is so easy to overestimate children's abilities, or move them on before learning has been properly consolidated. Many – perhaps most – will already have the early behaviours in Checklist 1. But some may not, and the only way of knowing for sure which is which, and exactly which behaviours they do have, is by observing each child individually.

This need not be as onerous and time-consuming as it seems. The checklists provide a quick and simple way of recording individual progress. As each child exhibits a behaviour or question form confidently, competently and consistently, it is ticked off on the checklist. This should not be on the basis of a single occasion. Each behaviour or question form needs to be consistent – repeated and reliable – as well as confident and competent.

Staff may want to wait until the end of the week before reviewing all the children in their group and bringing the checklists up to date. The best test is whether children are showing a behaviour spontaneously, outside of small-group teaching. Behaviour should not be assessed on the basis of small-group work alone, and if there is any doubt about a particular behaviour it should not be credited. It is always better to underestimate children's abilities than overestimate them. Note too that at this level the test is whether children are actually using the relevant question form: that is, can ask that question in appropriate circumstances, not just answer it or copy others.

Staff also need to be sure that children are not just demonstrating that behaviour as a result of the week's teaching but have properly consolidated it. There can be considerable variation, from child to child and from skill to skill, in how long it takes to consolidate new learning. Most children consolidate new skills easily and naturally through normal classroom experience, but those who were slow to establish a skill in the first place are also likely to need longer to consolidate it.

Staff should also make a note of any behaviours that have proved difficult so they can go over them again later in the term, and should allow time for this in their long-term planning. They may need to come back to some of them several times, especially with children in the Delayed group. They should also allow a couple of weeks at the beginning of each term to check the previous term's learning; and then repeat teaching of any items that children seem to have forgotten. It is always more important that children consolidate basic skills than that they move on to more advanced ones.

> ## KEY POINTS
>
> ● Each child is monitored separately using the checklists. As each child acquires a behaviour or question form it is ticked off on the checklist.
>
> ● A behaviour or question form should only be credited when the child is using it confidently, competently and consistently. If there is any doubt about a behaviour, it should not be credited.
>
> ● Staff need to ensure that each behaviour or question form has been properly consolidated, and should return later to any items that have proved difficult, to confirm that previous learning has been retained.
>
> ● It is always more important that children consolidate basic skills than that they move on to more advanced ones.

Moving on

The class should normally keep working on the same few question forms on a rolling basis, until everyone – or almost everyone – has learnt them. As each question form is learnt, the teacher can include another one, and so on through the checklist. Each small group, similarly, works on the same few behaviours until everyone in that group has learnt them. It does not matter if some children are learning more quickly than others. It is always better to consolidate than push ahead too soon; all children will benefit from the extra practice; and if some of them can do some things comfortably, the others may be able to learn from them. Teachers sometimes think they need to keep changing material or activities to retain children's interest and extend their experience, but even at this age children like to repeat things and will always benefit from it, particularly if they are having difficulty with the language that goes with it.

There may, however, come a time when a group or the class just has to move on, because some children are becoming bored or frustrated, or are showing signs of stress or anxiety at the constant repetition. This might be a good time to reorganise teaching groups, or a group can come back to the same items later on, by which time the children having difficulty may be more ready for them. It is a good idea in any case to repeat any items that have proved difficult, as a way of reinforcing and consolidating everyone's learning as well as providing further support for those who need it.

Each group can go at its own pace but it may also be convenient to keep the class more or less together. Intervention needs to be differentiated, to meet the needs of different children, but it also needs to be manageable. If one group has completed a particular skill the teacher may want to mark time with them while she gives more attention to the other groups that are still working on it. Alternatively, she can let each group move on as soon as they are ready, but this will mean that different groups are working on different skills, and that some groups may complete the checklist well before others.

Either way, it is much easier to manage if the class is working on only one checklist at a time. The teacher should continue working on the same checklist until everyone – or almost everyone – has completed it. There may still be some children who are simply not ready to move on with the rest. They might really need to keep working on the same few behaviours, but if they do they will only fall further and further behind. Depending on resources, it may be possible to keep them together for specialist small-group work, or provide some additional personal support.

Each checklist is expected to take more than a term to complete so, allowing for the time needed for initial screening at the beginning of the year and for any preliminary work on Listening Skills, Narrative Skills is almost certain to extend into the second year of primary school (children aged six to seven). This is why Narrative Skills is presented as a two-year programme, though it will still benefit all children even if it can only be used for a single year. But what matters more than how far anyone gets is that everyone acquires the more basic skills before being expected to master more advanced ones.

It is, however, impossible to be precise about any of this. One size is not going to fit all, and teachers will need to use their own experience and judgement in deciding when and how to move on from one behaviour, skill or checklist to the next.

KEY POINTS

- The class normally keeps working on the same question forms on a rolling basis until everyone has learnt them.

- Each group normally keeps working on the same skill until everyone has learnt all the behaviours, but it may sometimes be better to move on to another skill and come back to that one again later, or to reorganise the teaching groups.

- Each group can go at its own pace through the checklist but staff should wait until all groups have completed that checklist before proceeding to the next checklist.

- Special arrangements may have to be made for children or groups that are having particular difficulty.

- Each checklist is expected to take more than a term to complete.

Links to literacy

Narrative skills are particularly important for writing. Formal writing requires two skills: the ability to put your thoughts into a coherent form (narrative), and the ability to present those thoughts using physical marks. Teaching tends to focus on the second of these – the motor skill – and take the first for granted. But before they can write coherently and at any length children need to be able to talk coherently and at length. They need the vocabulary to express a range of ideas; they need the grammatical structures to express these ideas coherently; and they need to be able to remember those thoughts and put them in a coherent order.

Schools are currently under considerable pressure to introduce children to writing as soon as possible, but many children are simply not ready for it. Children who find extended talking difficult will find writing equally difficult, whether or they have the physical skills: if they cannot say it, how can they be expected to write it? Children should not be expected to write about current activities, much less about the past or the future, until they are able to talk about them fluently. Teachers should always check that children show the relevant skill in their spoken language – telling a coherent story, talking about what will or might happen – before expecting them to produce it in their written work. Boys in particular seem much more willing to write about something if they have been able to talk about it first.

On top of that, independent writing often begins in the wrong place. Children are asked to write a sentence, or write down their 'news'. But writing a sentence, as such, is a pointless, even meaningless, exercise. Adults seldom write 'a sentence', just for the sake of it, and many children do even not understand what a sentence is. It adds an unnecessary linguistic burden to what is already a difficult task. So does writing their 'news', which is past-tense writing that many children find difficult.

Independent writing should begin instead with simple exercises that are enjoyable and meaningful, and make as few demands as possible on children's grammatical and narrative skills: writing names, addresses, labels for boxes, shelves or cupboards, lists of friends or family, what they want for birthday or Christmas presents, or what they need to take with them on holiday. These simple tasks allow children to practise the motor skill – writing letter shapes – without making demands on their linguistic competence.

The teacher can then introduce more extended writing such as messages, directions and instructions, recipes, questions and answers, or notes to friends. Writing these things on a computer may be more fun – and seem more natural – than writing them down on paper, but notes and messages can be 'mailed' to each other or displayed on a bulletin board. Finally, children should be able to write descriptions of themselves, their friends or where they live, before being expected to write 'news' or stories. The text box suggests some early writing tasks relating to the three Narrative Skills checklists.

SOME EARLY WRITING TASKS

These writing tasks should not be introduced in parallel with the checklists, but only when children have fully mastered the relevant spoken skills: they should not be expected to do something in their writing that they cannot do easily in their talk.

The 'Writing in the Present' tasks should be appropriate for children aged 5 to 6, but 'Writing about the Past' will be more appropriate for children aged 6 to 7, and 'Writing about the Future' will be for children who have completed all three checklists.

Writing in the Present

labels, signs, captions, lists, etc.

simple texts like invitations, messages or notes

answers to simple questions like 'Who is this?', 'What are they doing?', 'Where are they?'

simple descriptions of themselves, their family, the school, etc.

Writing about the Past

simple descriptions of recent personal experiences

simple accounts of recent events like a school trip

simple accounts of familiar stories

Writing about the Future

simple accounts of something that will happen, like what they will do tomorrow

requests, e.g. for information for topic work, or materials for craft work

endings for unfinished stories

These and other activities are described in more detail in Chapter 10 of the *Activities Handbook* in *Teaching Talking* (Locke and Beech, 2005).

At the same time children should be developing other literacy-support skills, including:

- Awareness, understanding and use of reading: Staff should be talking to children about when and why we want to read things, not just for pleasure but for many practical purposes. Younger children (aged five to six) should be getting familiar with other types of written account besides stories, such as factual writing, information sources and poetry. Older children (aged six to seven) should be getting familiar with different types of written material besides books, such as signs, letters/emails, magazines, websites, and instruction manuals. They should also be learning to summarise and abstract information (simple comprehension exercises), and getting to know the technical vocabulary of books and reading, such as words like 'sentence', 'capital letter', 'full stop', 'noun', 'verb', 'writer/author', 'title' and 'page number'.

- Auditory and phonic skills: At this age children need to extend their auditory memories beyond learning rhymes and songs into learning simple factual items by heart, such as the days of the week, the months of the year, or number bonds. They should also be using a phonics programme to extend their knowledge of word sounds, for reading, writing and spelling. Younger children (aged five to six) should be learning to link single letters to their sound and sounds to single letters; learning how to sound out simple three-letter words; and be beginning to use this knowledge in their reading and writing. Older children (aged six to seven) should be learning to do this with four-letter words and with letter combinations like *sh-, ch-* or *-ing*, sound blends like *bl-, br-* or *sw-*, and vowel pairs like *oo, ar, ea* ('leaf'), *ay* and *ow* ('how').

- Visual-motor skills: By this stage visual-motor work will need to concentrate on the mechanics of writing: letter formation, sizing, and spacing for younger children (aged five to six); punctuation, use of cases, paragraphing and simple layout for older children (aged six to seven).

- Awareness, understanding and use of writing: This is most easily developed by preparing children for the different writing tasks listed above. At the same time they should be making use of written sources like wall-charts or displays for their own writing, and taking a more informed interest in the writing of others: for example, suggesting captions or formats.

Child's name	Band 1	Is asking questions of several different types	Can talk about what is happening in a picture scene or story	Can talk about what they are currently doing	Band 2	Can talk about something they have done in the past	Can talk about a familiar DVD or TV programme	Can describe what happened in a story	*Competent*	*Developing*	*Delayed*
_____											
_____											
_____											
_____											
_____											
_____											
_____											
_____											
_____											
_____											
_____											
_____											
_____											
_____											
_____											
_____											
_____											
_____											

● Children who lack any of the behaviours in Band 1 are identified as Delayed, even if they have some of the behaviours in Band 2.

● Children who have all the behaviours in Band 1 but lack any of the behaviours in Band 2 are identified as Developing.

● Children who have all the behaviours in both Bands are identified as Competent.

Child's name

Question forms

												Can ask *What's that?*
												Can ask *What's it for?*
												Can ask *Is it.......?*
												Can ask *Where is....?*
												Can ask *Who is....-ing?*
												Can ask *What is/are .... doing?*
												Can ask *Do/Does.......?*

Describing the present

												Can talk about what is happening in a picture scene, using nouns and verbs
												Can describe what is happening in a picture scene, using adjectives, adverbs and prepositions
												Can talk about what they are currently doing
												Can talk about what other children are doing
												Can describe themselves and other children, e.g. what they are wearing
												Can relate picture scenes and stories to their own experience
												Can talk about the feelings of people in a story

Sequencing

												Can put a sequence of three to four pictures into the right order
												Can tell a story using a three to four picture sequence
												Can explain why the sequence of pictures is correct
												Can give a series of simple directions or instructions
												Can describe a familiar sequence of events in the right order
												Uses sequence markers like *now, then, before, after, next*

One Step at a Time

Child's name

Question forms

Can ask *Did......?*
Can ask *Was/Were......?*
Can ask *Has/Have......?*
Can ask *When?*
Can ask *Why?*
Can ask *How many/how much......?*

Describing the past

Can describe what has just happened
Can describe a recent event, e.g. what happened yesterday
Can describe something that they did in the recent past
Can describe how they made or did something
Can talk about a recent TV programme or familiar DVD
Can retell a story, with help
Can retell a story, without help

Sequencing

Can describe events in the right order
Can talk about what could have happened earlier in a picture scene or story
Uses past tense correctly and consistently
Uses time markers like *the other day, once, yesterday, before correctly*
Can identify the key points in a past account
Can begin and end a past account appropriately

Teaching Speaking and Listening © Ann Locke (Bloomsbury Publishing plc, 2013)

Child's name												

Question forms

												Can ask *Will......?*
												Can ask *How?*
												Can ask *Whose?*
												Can ask *Which?*

Describing the future

												Can say what is about to happen in a familiar situation
												Can say what is about to happen in a story or picture sequence
												Can give a simple first-person account of what they are going to do next
												Can describe what is needed to do or make something, e.g. craft or cooking
												Can describe a familiar future event or activity, e.g. what will happen at the weekend
												Can anticipate the outcome of a simple experiment
												Can suggest an ending for an unfamiliar story, or a new ending for a familiar story

Sequencing

												Can describe what they are about to make or do
												Can talk about what might happen next in a story or picture sequence
												Can talk about what might be going to happen in a familiar TV series
												Uses the future tense correctly and consistently
												Uses time markers like *soon*, *later*, *tomorrow*, *next week*, correctly

Narrative skills — Vocabulary wordlist — One Step at a Time

Quality	Colour	Texture	Sound	Shape	Size	Quantity	Number	Space	Time	Movement	Feelings and emotion
clear	bright	furry	higher	border	height	almost	double	apart	afternoon	beat	beautiful
heaviest	cream	prickly	hushed	corner	huge	altogether	even	beginning	autumn	exercise	brave
hollow	light	uneven	lower	curved	largest	equal	odd	centre	evening	fastest	comfortable
older	purple		softly	edge	length	fewest	quarter	clockwise	hour	freely	excited/exciting
solid	scarlet			face	longer	only		direction	minute	jerky	feelings
				narrow	shortest	part		end	month	quickest	glad
				oval	size	several		left	morning	slowest	greedy
				pyramid	smaller			opposite	season	rhythm	lazy
				shallow	thick			right	spring		nasty
				slanted	tiny			row	time		scared
				slope	width			upright	tomorrow		shy
				sphere					week		surprised/surprising
				symmetrical					year		upset
				wide					yesterday		worried

Teaching Speaking and Listening © Ann Locke (Bloomsbury Publishing plc, 2013)

NOTES ON CHECKLIST 1

Talking about the present

Most children entering school have a grasp of past, present and future and are reasonably fluent in the use of verb tenses, including irregular forms like *found*, *went* or *did*. But they are likely to be hesitant or inconsistent in their use of tenses when talking at any length, and many will be poor at sequencing events into a coherent sequence. This checklist aims to develop children's skills in talking about current events and activities before going on to accounts of the past or future. This does not mean that talk about the past or the future should be discouraged or avoided. On the contrary, any correct or appropriate use should be encouraged and praised. But the first checklist focuses on the present.

Question forms

Note that the emphasis here is on asking questions: on using a question form appropriately, to find out something you want to know. This can be practised in circle-time and partner work by getting children to take turns to ask each other the question of the week. They may simply copy one another at first, even taking turns to ask each other the very same question. But ultimately they need to know how to use the various question forms to find things out, so they need to do more than simply mouth the words. It is also important that their question gets an answer, and that they listen to what the answer is. Using the questions table with a range of different objects and pictures is a good way of working on these skills.

The first three question forms – *What's that?*, *What's it for?* and *Is it…?* – are about what things are or are like. They can feature one at a time as 'question of the week' but will usually overlap and get worked on together. Games like 'I spy' and 'Twenty questions', suitably simplified, are good ways of teaching *Is it…?*

Where is…? can be taught using objects in the classroom – 'Where is the blackboard?', 'Where is the door?', 'Where is the window?' – or having pictures for children to ask each other about. *Who is …. -ing?*, and *What is/are they doing?* are about what people are doing so they will overlap and get worked on together, by using pictures of people in different occupations or doing different or unusual things.

Do/Does? can be taught by taking it in turns to ask questions like 'Do you like ice-cream?', 'Do you have a dog?', 'Do you go shopping with your mum?'. A variant which children may find more exciting is the game 'Silly questions' where they ask each other silly things like 'Do you like spiders?', 'Do you eat flowers?', 'Do you go to bed with your shoes on?'.

Children will find the second person *Do you?* easier than the third person *Does she?* but this should be introduced to both forms. In circle-time, they can ask each other different questions: 'Do you like ice-cream?', 'Do you like swimming?', and then go round again asking 'Does Tracey like ice-cream?', 'Does Lok like swimming?'

For more detailed suggestions for small-group activities see Chapter 5 of the Activities Handbook in *Teaching Talking* (Locke and Beech, 2005).

Describing the present

This section focuses on developing more expanded and more detailed descriptions of things and people, including accounts of what is implicit in a picture or story. Staff will need to assemble a collection of photographs or picture scenes for children to talk about in small-group work, ranging from simple and familiar to more complex and less familiar scenes. If the scenes are complicated or unusual at first, children may not know where or how to start describing them, but as they get more confident and familiar with the task they should be able to handle more complex material.

The first two items are relatively simple and should be well within the range of most five-year-olds. The second asks for more complex constructions: not just 'a ball' or 'a car', but 'a big red ball', 'the car is going fast', 'he's fallen over', 'she's talking loudly', 'he's very greedy, eating all the sausages', etc. Children can then be asked to describe themselves or other children. Relating events to their own experience – 'Have you ever fallen over like that?' – can help them understand what the characters in a story are feeling, or why they behave as they do.

The teacher may need to provide 'pointer' questions to help children develop increasingly detailed descriptions: 'Who's this in the picture?', 'Where are they?', 'What are they doing?', 'Why do you think they're doing that?'. The same questions can be used again and again in different contexts, and even be written out so children can refer to them and follow them through when working in their pairs. This may seem unduly mechanistic and repetitive but young children tend to be disorganised and unsystematic in their accounts of things and learning to consider a series of questions in order will help them to think and describe things more coherently.

For more detailed suggestions for small-group activities see Chapter 6 of the Activities Handbook in *Teaching Talking* (Locke and Beech, 2005).

Sequencing

This section focuses on children's ability to give a coherent, structured description of things or events in the right order. They will find this much more difficult than merely talking about them, so it is best to start with very simple or very familiar sequences such as photos of the children themselves during a classroom or domestic routine. A particularly good place to start is with series of photos taken of – and even by – the children themselves during familiar classroom or domestic routines and activities.

They first need to be able to put the photos or cards in the right order; then report what is happening; and finally explain why this order is the right one, which can be tested by putting cards or photos in the wrong order and seeing if they can say why it is wrong. Children may find sequencing cards, in particular, very puzzling at first, and may need to watch others and have the procedure explained several times before they grasp what it is they need to do.

The next item is for them to give other children a series of instructions, such as where to find or put things, how to play a game, or how to clean out the classroom pet's cage. A sequence of events is a series of events that happen in a particular order, as in getting up, getting dressed and having breakfast, going to the swimming pool, or what happens at a birthday party. Here too, the teacher may need to provide 'pointer' questions to guide children: 'How do you go back home after school?', 'Who do you go with?', 'Which way do you go?', 'What do you do when you get home?'.

By the time they can do all this children should be using simple sequencing terms like *now*, *then*, *before*, *after*, *first* and *next*, but these may sometimes need to be taught explicitly. The teacher can use group work or circle-time to ask what *before* or *next* mean, discuss the answers, and then get children to give each other a sentence using that word.

NOTES ON CHECKLIST 2

Talkling about the past

This checklist extends children's narrative skills into accounts of the past. They should not find it difficult to describe past events, but may have more difficulty in putting them in sequence.

Question forms

Did...?, *Was...?*, *Were...?*, *Has...?*, *Have...?* and *When...?* all lend themselves to circle-time and partner work: 'Did you go shopping/watch TV/have eggs for dinner?'; 'Were you outside/late for school/eating your lunch?'; 'Have you got a dog/read your book/been on a train?'; 'When did you go to bed/clean your teeth/see your grandma?'. Some also lend themselves to 'Silly questions': 'Did you eat any grass yesterday?', 'Have you got an elephant?'.

Children will find the second person *Were you?* and *Have you?* easier than the third person *Was he?* or *Has she?* A good way of teaching *Was?* is to get children to ask questions about a familiar story: 'Was that a bad wolf?', 'Was Little Red Riding Hood scared?', etc. Stories can also be used to teach *Did?*: 'Did Cinderella have a pretty dress?', 'Did the prince find her?'.

Why? can be taught using a set of pictures showing different incidents so children can ask each other 'Why is the boy crying?', 'Why is the cat hiding?', etc. *How many?* and *How much?* are most conveniently taught in maths and science lessons or in practical activities like cooking.

For more detailed suggestions for small-group activities see Chapter 5 of the Activities Handbook in *Teaching Talking* (Locke and Beech, 2005).

Describing the past

The first three items are again very simple and should be well within the range of most five-year-olds. 'Just happened' means the immediate past. 'Recent' means in the last few days, depending on how memorable it is. A good way of teaching these items is to have 'review' sessions where children describe what they have been doing during the day or what they have just been learning. This will reinforce that learning and develop questioning as well as other skills. When they are familiar with this sort of exercise they can do review work in their groups or with their talking partner.

Children are likely to find it easier to talk about what happened to, or was done by, someone else than to talk about things they have done themselves. They may also find it easier to talk about a favourite TV programme or DVD than about real events. Retelling a story, even a familiar one, is likely to be even more difficult.

For more detailed suggestions for small group activities see Chapter 7 of the Activities Handbook in *Teaching Talking* (Locke and Beech, 2005).

Sequencing

Retelling a story is a familiar classroom exercise but children may get more excited about retelling a TV programme or a favourite DVD. The aim here is to help children to be more systematic and structured in doing it: putting events in the right order without going into excessive detail, or providing an appropriate beginning and ending rather than starting or ending in the middle of things. They should also be able to keep to the correct tense reasonably consistently, and not wander erratically from the past to the present or even the future; and have some idea of which pronouns to use to identify different people, and when they need to repeat who they are talking about.

Staff may need to work on these items at a whole-class level for some weeks before getting children to work on them with a partner. Once children are able to give a reasonably detailed account staff can help them summarise by asking what are the important things that happened. Depending on the example, they might ask 'What are the clever things that boy did?', or 'What did the dog do that was difficult?', and so on; or they might just ask what were the main or most important things that happened. They should also check that children know how to start and end their narratives.

NOTES ON CHECKLIST 3

Talking about the future

This checklist extends narrative skills into descriptions of the future. Children are likely to find this more difficult than talking about the present or the past. Most classroom activities provide opportunities to talk about the past and the present, but staff may have to devise opportunities to talk about what is going to happen.

Question forms

These questions lend themselves to circle-time and partner-work: 'Will it rain tomorrow?', 'How do you mix the paints?', 'Whose shoe is this?', 'Which is your bag?', and so on. *How?*, *Whose?* and *Which?* can be taught using objects or pictures: 'How did he do that?', 'Whose bag is black?', 'Which car is the best?', etc. *Which?* can also be taught in science lessons: 'Which of these is the quickest/smallest/heaviest?'.

Describing the future

These items are relatively straightforward to teach but children may find some of them difficult, especially having to say what might happen or inventing the end to a story. To help them with this they need to be given frequent opportunities during stories and classroom lessons or demonstrations to talk about what they think is going to happen, with the teacher suggesting possible alternative outcomes. They can also be given anticipation games, where they try to guess what is going to happen next in a picture sequence or a story, and asked to discuss their suggestions with one another.

A pictorial weekly timetable in a prominent position in the classroom, with symbols or pictures illustrating different lessons or activities, can be a useful teaching aid. At the start of each day children can discuss that day's lessons and activities, first with the teacher, then with their partner. When they have become used to this they can talk about not just what they are going to do but also what they need for it and how they will start. This introduces them to planning as well as sequencing.

Sequencing

The most important and most common form of future tense sequencing is planning a future activity. Children can be introduced to this by being asked to discuss something they are going to make or do: what they will need, the order they will need to do it in, and so on. 'Plan, Do and Review' is a useful exercise that can be part of any lesson, and part of most teaching. As well as reinforcing learning, 'Plan' promotes talk about the future, and 'Review' promotes talk about the past.

Chapter 11 Discussion Skills

Discussion Skills is a programme for developing thinking skills, learning skills, social understanding and emotional literacy in children aged seven or over but can be used with older children of any age, up to and including secondary school. It is intended for children who have done Narrative Skills and are thoroughly familiar with partner work. If a significant number of children have not had this experience, it is recommended that the whole class does some Narrative Skills work before beginning Discussion Skills. Partly to allow for this, and because the skills it develops are open-ended, Discussion Skills is expected to extend across at least two years but will still benefit all children where it can only be used for a single year.

Discussion can be thought of as extended and expanded conversation. The rules are much the same: we take turns as speaker and listener, listen and respond to what others say and keep to a topic, or change it in an acceptable way. But discussion typically involves more people than conversation, stays on the same themes for longer, and requires both extended listening and extended speaking. Participants may have to listen to and remember a complex sequence of ideas before producing their own extended response. Discussion also tends to be both more general and more abstract. Whereas conversation tends to be about particular events and activities, discussion tends to involve ideas and opinions.

This is a highly effective but under-utilised means of teaching and learning. It allows children to learn from other children as well as from teachers, and encourages them to find things out for themselves. Like adults, children learn best if they can be in control of their learning, active rather than passive. They can do this by talking to the teacher or other children about what they know already, what they need to know and how they can find it out, and then about what they have discovered. It is much easier for them to reflect on what they know or have learnt through talking to other children, helping each other, than having to do it on their own.

Discussion also develops children's thinking skills. It is, in effect, thinking out loud, and talking something through is often easier than silent thought, for children as for adults. In discussion, children have to formulate their own ideas and opinions and subject them to the judgement of others. They sometimes have to clarify, explain or justify what they are saying; consider other people's ideas and opinions, clarify and evaluate them; and even adjust or modify their own views in the light of what they have heard. This includes exploring and debating ideas that aren't right or wrong, correct or incorrect, but a matter of opinion, where people can have different points of view. Some schools have introduced philosophy for children, not because they expect to turn children into mature philosophers but because it provides an opportunity to discuss more abstract ideas, express personal opinions, and think things through by talking about them.

At the same time, discussion helps to develop children's understanding of other people. They don't just learn from others; they learn about them, their interests, needs and wants as well as their opinions, attitudes and points of view. They learn to take other people's perspective, to understand and accept different points of view and, when interests conflict, they have to learn to negotiate, reach agreement and, if necessary, compromise.

Discussion can also be used to develop children's ability to identify, describe and explain their feelings and emotions, for themselves as well as others. This is an important part of what is sometimes called emotional literacy: the ability to recognise, manage and communicate your own thoughts, feelings and behaviour, and to interpret and respond to the emotions and actions of others. These are difficult and complex matters that we spend most of our lives trying to understand, but it is increasingly recognised that schools should be giving more attention to this aspect of children's development. They are important social skills and children need to be helped to understand them at a level appropriate to their experience.

Discussion Skills can be used with children at any age from seven onwards, up to and including secondary school. It is primarily intended for children who have already done Narrative Skills and are thoroughly familiar both with partner work and with talking in detail about the future as well as about the present and past. In a class where a significant number of children have not had this experience, or did not complete the previous level, it is recommended that they all have some practice with narrative skills first, before beginning Discussion Skills. How much work they will need on Narrative Skills will depend on their age, ability and confidence. A class of seven-year-olds who have not done Narrative Skills should work through the third checklist, or even the second and third, before attempting Discussion Skills. Older children may not need to do much more than practise partner work as described in Chapter 10. Partly to give this flexibility, and because the skills it develops are open-ended, Discussion Skills is expected to extend across at least two years. But it will still benefit all children even if it can only be used for a single year, and they do not complete all the programme.

Children who have completed Discussion Skills should be more able to think independently, and direct and control their own learning. They will be more confident in talking with, and to, a group of children and, as a result, will have developed better communication, listening and social skills. They will be able to work with other children without adult support, to prepare, plan, predict, explain and solve problems. They will be more aware of feelings in themselves and in others, and better able to explain or justify their own behaviour or give reasons and respond to the reasons of others. They will be willing to explore and resolve disagreements through talk.

Discussion work

The only practicable way to develop and assess children's discussion skills is through small-group discussion work. Whole-class discussion can only involve a few children at a time, and probably only those who already have the best discussion skills. Small-group discussion work may seem impractical at first, but like partner work in Narrative Skills it is a valuable teaching tool in its own right. It can be used to deliver any part of the curriculum and quickly becomes an integral part of everyday classroom practice. It takes pressure off staff by allowing children to work independently. It boosts the confidence and general language skills of anxious or less able children. It can provide the extra practice, consolidation and generalisation that children need but is difficult to achieve in schools. It can even ensure that all children get to practise their discussion skills each and every day. It enables children to learn from and support each other as well as learning from their teacher, something our education system does not encourage often enough. And children enjoy it.

Independent small-group discussion may seem daunting and potentially disruptive at first but teachers should not be afraid to 'let go'. There tend to be two main concerns: that it will be too noisy, and that children will not stay on topic. Experience does not support either concern: 'It's amazing what children can do when you put them to it!'. Noise should not be a problem if, for example, children are told to use a 'small' voice for small-group discussion and keep their 'big' voice in whole-class lessons; and they will usually remain on topic provided the task is clear and appropriate, within their capabilities, and not allowed to go on for too long.

The Discussion Skills programme will help children develop the skills they need to benefit fully from this way of working. However, many children will find independent discussion work difficult at first, and it may be necessary to spend several weeks at the beginning of the year – possibly even into the second term – familiarising them with discussion at a whole-class level, and in partner work, before introducing independent discussion in small groups. It is also crucial that the topics for discussion are kept simple and within children's capabilities, especially at first.

Initial screening

The initial screen helps teachers:

- 'tune-in' to the relevant skills at this level of the programme
- identify children's current development of these skills
- determine the amount of support they are likely to need.

The first of these may be the most important. For Discussion Skills teachers need to be aware of children's ability to use language for a number of different educational and social purposes: to share knowledge and find things out, to explain, plan and problem solve, and to reach agreement. They need to be aware of children's ability to listen properly to each other, respond appropriately, or modify their own views accordingly. They also need to be aware of the differences in these skills between children, so they can provide the targeted support that is needed. Which children contribute to a discussion? Say almost nothing? Respond but don't initiate? Can keep to the topic? Notice if someone hasn't understood them? Can explain what they mean? In different words, or do they just repeat themselves?

All this can be more difficult than it might seem. Teachers may not be used to discriminating these behaviours, or identifying them in individual children. These are the skills they need to develop, and the screening process can help them do it.

The initial screen is a quick and simple measure, not a formal assessment. It identifies children as:

- Competent: they seem to be acquiring these skills without too much difficulty and are not expected to need special attention.

- Developing: they seem to be slower in acquiring these skills and are likely to need some support and attention.

- Delayed: they seem to be having difficulty in acquiring these skills and are likely to need more intensive support and attention.

These groupings are intended to be flexible and are likely to change in the course of a term or year.

Screening should not be carried out until children are working comfortably in their discussion groups, which also gives the class teacher time to observe individual children informally and gauge some idea of their current skills. The screen can then be completed, with a colleague if possible. Even at this age children's behaviour can be variable and a second opinion is always useful. It is also easy to take some of these behaviours for granted, or underestimate the skills of quiet children and overestimate the skills of more talkative ones.

Each child needs to be considered separately. Teachers are often surprised to discover that while it seems 'the whole class' can do something there are actually huge variations in what individual children contribute and their level of detail or accuracy.

It is also important to consider each behaviour separately. A behaviour should only be credited if a child is using it confidently, competently and consistently. If there is any doubt or disagreement, the behaviour should not be credited. It is always better to underestimate children's abilities than overestimate them.

The initial screen has two bands, and children are assessed band by band. That is, if they do not have all the behaviours in Band 1, they do not need to be assessed on Band 2.

- Children who lack any of the behaviours in Band 1 are identified as Delayed, even if they have some of the behaviours in Band 2.

- Children who have all the behaviours in Band 1 but lack any of the behaviours in Band 2 are identified as Developing.

- Children who have all the behaviours in both bands are identified as Competent.

The Delayed group may include some children with special educational needs but should not be thought of as a special needs group. Children can be delayed for all sorts of reasons, including lack of confidence, lack of experience, or lack of familiarity with the English language; and some children with special needs may have perfectly adequate language skills, or show uneven patterns of development. Children with special needs may need extra support but should be included in the *One Step* programme in the same way as any other child. For further guidance see Appendix 1.

KEY POINTS

- While children are getting used to working in discussion groups the teacher can be observing them informally, focusing on the behaviours to be assessed.

- Working with a colleague if possible, the class teacher completes the initial screen for each child separately.

- A behaviour should be credited only if a child is using it competently, confidently and consistently. If there is any doubt or disagreement, or the behaviour is hesitant or infrequent, it should not be credited.

- The screen has two bands, and children are assessed band by band: if they do not have all the behaviours in Band 1, they do not need to be assessed on Band 2.

- Children who lack any of the behaviours in Band 1 are identified as Delayed, even if they have some of the behaviours in Band 2.

- Children who have all the behaviours in Band 1 but lack any of the behaviours in Band 2 are identified as Developing.

- Children who have all the behaviours in both bands are identified as Competent.

Skills checklist

Discussion Skills uses three skills checklists to focus and guide classroom intervention and monitor individual progress:

- Learning through discussion
- Planning and problem solving
- Negotiation and emotional literacy.

Each checklist consists of a number of distinct behaviours or sub-skills grouped together under a few broad types of skill. The first checklist, for example, is divided into Basic discussion skills and Extending knowledge. The Basic discussion skills include waiting your turn, keeping to the topic, and being able to clarify what you have said if others have not understood you. It will be convenient to refer to each group of items as a skill and the separate items as behaviours.

These skills and behaviours are listed in rough developmental order as a guide to intervention. Different children will of course show different patterns of development, and some of them – especially those identified as Competent – will have some or all of the behaviours already or be able to establish them almost immediately. But others may need to learn them one by one.

The teacher normally works through each checklist in sequence, a few behaviours at a time, starting with the first few behaviours under Basic discussion skills. She looks for these behaviours as children work in their discussion groups, paying particular attention to any children identified as Delayed. If a child is finding a behaviour difficult, she can work with him on it then and there.

Behaviours that go together get learnt together; in working on one, the teacher will often have been introducing another; and this provides an easy transition from one behaviour to the next. Some children will show some or all of the relevant behaviours already, or be able to establish them almost immediately. Others may need to establish them slowly, one by one.

Each behaviour is, however, assessed separately. Teachers need to be confident that each child has established it, and the only way to be sure of that is to work through the checklists systematically, ticking them off one by one.

KEY POINTS

- Each checklist identifies two or three general skills, divided into separate behaviours or sub-skills.

- Skills and behaviours are listed in rough developmental order as a guide to intervention.

- The teacher normally works through each checklist in sequence, a few behaviours at a time.

- Every child and every behaviour needs to be assessed and monitored separately.

Classroom intervention

Discussion skills are taught through a combination of whole-class work, small-group discussion and targeted intervention with individual children. The checklists set specific objectives for all children on a rolling basis, while the initial screens help determine the amount of support needed for each child. Detailed advice on intervention for specific skills and behaviours is given in the Notes to each checklist.

Whole-class work

Whole-class work is used to introduce and explain discussion work in general and small-group discussion in particular, and to explain and introduce specific discussion topics and/or specific discussion skills.

The teacher can start by asking her class what they understand by 'discussion', and then discuss with them why it is useful, how it works and what the rules are. She can then summarise their contributions, something like this:

> 'Discussion helps us learn things. We can get good ideas from other people. We can find out things we didn't know, and tell other people things they didn't know. It can help us solve problems and avoid arguments. But we need to listen to what others are saying and wait till they have finished.'

All this is worth repeating several times over the first few weeks and at regular intervals thereafter. Even when children have begun working in their discussion groups, this more general explanation will help them to reflect on what they are doing, why, and how well it is working.

The teacher will next need to explain and demonstrate discussion work itself, by choosing a topic and a set of questions and discussing them with a few children in front of the rest of the class. Again, she may have to do this several times before getting them to try discussion on their own, without support. Since they should already be familiar with partner work she can set it as a partner exercise at first, before putting pairs together to form groups of four, and then groups of six.

Each specific discussion topic will also need to be introduced at the whole-class level: the teacher should explain the topic to her class, why she wants them to discuss it, and what they need to do in their discussion groups. She may also need to explain how they should work at it together: for example, when it gets to problem solving, or agreement and compromise, they may need to be told that this is not about being right or wrong, but about considering different opinions and learning from them.

Finally, she may want to explain what it is, specifically, that she is looking for in this piece of discussion work: for example, whether they are listening to each other, or trying out different suggestions, or adjusting their views in the light of what other children say. Children are much more likely to work productively together and demonstrate the appropriate skills if they know exactly what is expected of them and what they should be expecting from each other.

Small-group discussion

Each discussion group should ideally be no more than six children, though the number of groups may also depend on the space available to put groups in different places where they will not disturb each other. Children who are very talkative should not be grouped together because they are likely to dominate and not allow other children the practice they need. Competent children can be grouped with Developing children, and Developing children with Delayed, but it is not usually a good idea to put Competent children with Delayed. Groupings can be varied from time to time.

At first, while children are getting used to this way of working, teachers need to avoid overloading them with new topics, and may have to set the same or similar topics over several days. But once they have become familiar with small-group discussion work, there is no reason why they should not be set two or three different topics each day, chosen from different parts of the curriculum.

A good way of providing whole-class feedback is to have a 'hot seat': at the end of each discussion session a child sits in the hot seat and tells the rest of the class what he and his group have been doing. The teacher can then use this as a way of developing the topic further with all children in the class.

Individual intervention

While children are working in their discussion groups, the teacher can move from group to group, paying particular attention to any children identified as Delayed. If a child is not showing a behaviour she is currently looking for, she should work with him then and there, as described below under Teaching Method. If some children are having particular difficulty developing these skills they can be given more practice by being put to discuss a current topic with a single partner, pairing each child with a more able one. They should have this extra partner work at least once a day if possible.

A list of items currently being worked on should be displayed prominently in the classroom and given to parents, so everyone can see and refer to it and use it to guide their interaction with individual children.

KEY POINTS

- Whole-class work is used to

  - introduce and explain discussion work in general (what it is, why it is useful, how it works, what the rules are)

  - demonstrate and practise discussion work

  - introduce and explain each discussion topic

  - explain and demonstrate the specific aspects of discussion work currently being targeted.

- Children are assigned to discussion groups of up to six children on the basis of the initial screen. Using discussion work, it should be possible for all children to practise discussion skills almost every day.

- The teacher works with individual children in their discussion groups, paying particular attention to any children identified as Delayed, and helping them to develop any behaviours they may be missing.

- A list of items currently being worked on should be displayed prominently, so all adults can use it to guide their interaction with individual children.

Vocabulary work

Vocabulary work is mostly treated as an optional element in *One Step at a Time* but has a different role in Discussion Skills because the wordlist contains vocabulary that children will need to know for their discussion work. It consists of 100 key words, divided into Discussion vocabulary needed for Checklists 1 and 2, and Vocabulary of feelings and emotion needed for Checklist 3.

The 50-word Discussion vocabulary is divided into verbs and other words, mostly nouns and some adjectives. Teachers should begin working on this vocabulary as soon as they start discussion work. Most of these words should already be familiar to most children, and some have been included in the wordlists at previous levels. But it is important to establish that everyone does understand words like 'summarise', 'co-operate' or 'index' before setting discussion tasks that use these words. Children can be very skilled at appearing to understand when they do not fully grasp what is expected of them, and what looks like lack of interest or application may simply be a failure of communication.

The 50-word Vocabulary of feelings and emotion is divided into contrasting pairs that can usefully be taught together, and various single words. Teachers will be working through this vocabulary as they introduce different discussion topics as described in the Notes to Checklist 3.

Detailed advice on vocabulary work is given in Chapter 12.

Lesson planning

Teachers usually want to decide in advance what they are going to teach, when they are going to teach it and how they are going to teach it, so they can prepare lessons, select activities, gather resources, inform other staff, advise parents, and so on. But planning also needs to be flexible because some skills may take longer to learn than expected, and sometimes very much longer.

Lesson planning includes selecting objectives, selecting topics or activities, preparing materials, and allocating times. The skills checklists provide teaching and learning objectives for all children. Suggestions for appropriate topics and questions for discussion are given in the Notes to each checklist. But it should not at first be necessary to plan separate discussion lessons or periods. Children can instead practise basic discussion skills in almost any lesson, discussing the various topics as and when they arise in the normal course of the curriculum. It is only later on, with more advanced skills like planning, negotiating, or discussing different emotions, that specific topics or lessons will need to be identified and planned for.

As well as identifying suitable topics for small-group discussion, the teacher will also need to plan which questions she is going to set, and any specific instructions she needs to give her class. Because children are going to have to work through these questions on their own, the questions should always be well within their experience and competence. If the topic is 'Rain', for example, the questions could include: 'Why do we need rain?', 'What happens if it rains too much?', 'What would happen if it didn't rain?', 'What can we do with the water?', 'How can we store it?'. If the topic is 'Caring for our pets', the questions could include: 'Why do we have pets?', 'How can we look after them?', 'What should we give them to eat?', 'Where do they sleep?', 'How much exercise do they need?'. And so on.

Teaching method

At this stage children are very largely teaching themselves or learning from each other. The simplest discussion skills, such as taking turns, keeping to a topic, or seeking and giving clarification, are the same as for conversation skills, and should be familiar to children from earlier steps in the programme, though they now need to be able to use them in wider contexts, over longer periods, and in larger groups. But more advanced skills, like summarising what they already know, explaining how something happened, or discussing the merits of a proposal, may be unfamiliar and need to be explained and demonstrated. As well as doing this with the class as a whole at the beginning of an exercise, the teacher will also need to work on specific skills with individual children in their discussion groups, helping them to do it.

The most effective teaching techniques are those that parents use to teach their children, usually without realising they are doing it (see Chapter 3):

● Highlighting: the adult draws attention to the relevant behaviour by discussing it, explaining its importance, or explaining how, when or why we do it: she might ask, for example, 'What should you do if you don't understand it?' or 'How can you help Joe understand what you mean?'. She can then discuss the responses and highlight the key points, explaining what clarification is and why we sometimes need to do it.

● Modelling: the adult illustrates the behaviour she wants children to learn: for example, she shows how to list steps in order, how to evaluate the success of a plan, or how to suggest improvements.

● Prompting: the adult encourages the child to respond, directing him towards the appropriate behaviour: 'Does that seem a good idea?', 'Why don't you think it's a good idea?'.

● Rewarding: the adult rewards any appropriate response with praise and further encouragement. Praise will be more effective if it can emphasise what was good about the response: 'That was a good clear explanation. Now I know how to make it!', 'That was a good idea you and Rabiya worked out together'. If a response is not quite what the adult is looking for, she can encourage a more appropriate one by asking questions, prompting, or modelling the behaviour again.

Suitable activities for teaching the different skills are suggested in the Notes to each checklist. If an activity is new the teacher should first demonstrate it and explain why they are doing it; and at the end of the session she should highlight what they have been doing, why they have been doing it, and how well it all went.

Monitoring progress

Continuing assessment of children's progress is crucial for effective teaching, particularly with spoken language where it is so easy to overestimate children's abilities, or move them on before learning has been properly consolidated. Many – perhaps most – of them will already have the behaviours in Checklist 1. But some may not, and the only way of knowing for sure which is which, and exactly which behaviours they do have, is by observing each child individually.

This need not be as onerous and time-consuming as it seems. The checklists provide a quick and simple way of recording individual progress. As each child exhibits a behaviour confidently, competently and consistently, it is ticked off on the checklist. This should not be on the basis of a single occasion. Each behaviour needs to be consistent – repeated and reliable – as well as confident and competent. The best test is whether a child is showing a behaviour spontaneously, and not just when the teacher has said she is looking for it. If there is any doubt about a particular behaviour, it should not be credited. It is always better to underestimate children's abilities than overestimate them.

There can also be considerable variation, from child to child and from skill to skill, in how long it takes to consolidate new learning. Most children consolidate new skills easily and naturally through normal classroom experience, but those who were slow to establish a skill in the first place are also likely to need longer to consolidate it. The teacher should make a note of any behaviours that individual children have found difficult, and go back over them again from time to time to check that previous learning has been retained. They may need to come back to some of them several times, especially with children identified as Delayed, and should allow for this in their long-term planning. The beginning of a new term is an obvious time to check learning from the previous term. It is always more important that children consolidate basic skills than that they move on to more advanced ones.

KEY POINTS

- Each child is monitored separately using the checklists. As each child acquires a behaviour it is ticked off on the checklist.

- A behaviour should only be credited when the child is using it confidently, competently and consistently. If there is any doubt about a behaviour, it should not be credited.

- The teacher needs to ensure that each behaviour has been properly consolidated, and should return later to any items that have proved difficult, to confirm that previous learning has been retained.

- It is always more important that children consolidate basic skills than that they move on to more advanced ones.

Moving on

In general, the teacher continues working on the same few behaviours with the children who need it until everyone has learnt them. She can then move on to the next few behaviours or the next skill, and so on through the checklist. By then, of course, other children will be demonstrating behaviours from even further down the checklist or from later checklists. This is all to the good, and she should encourage and support the use of any relevant skill. But her focus must always be on the slower children.

There may, however, come a time when she feels she just has to move on, because some children are becoming bored or frustrated, or are showing signs of stress or anxiety at the constant repetition. She can still come back to the same items later on, by which time the children having difficulty may be more ready for them. It is a good idea in any case to return to any items that have proved difficult, to reinforce and consolidate earlier learning.

The teacher will typically be working on different behaviours, and even different skills, with different children, but it will be very difficult to manage if she is trying to work on more than one checklist. Instead she should wait until everyone – or almost everyone – has completed the checklist before moving on to the next one. There may still be some children who are still simply not ready to move on with the rest. They really need to keep working on the same few behaviours, but if they do they will only fall further and further behind. Depending on resources, it may be possible to keep them together for specialist small-group work, or provide some additional personal support.

Each checklist is expected to take more than a term to complete so, allowing for the time needed to get the class used to small-group discussion and for any preliminary work on Narrative Skills, Discussion Skills is expected to extend across at least two years, though it will still benefit all children even if it can only be used for a single year. It is any case open-ended. Some of these skills are relatively simple, but others are quite complex, and many are themselves open-ended. They are skills we go on learning for the rest of our lives!

It is, however, impossible to be precise about any of this. One size is not going to fit all, and teachers will need to use their own experience and judgement in deciding when and how to move on from one behaviour, skill or checklist to the next.

KEY POINTS

- The teacher normally keeps working on the same behaviours until all children have learnt them, but it may sometimes be necessary to move on to the next skill or the next checklist. She may sometimes be working on different skills with different children, but should not attempt to work on two checklists at the same time.

- Each checklist is expected to take more than a term to complete.

Links to literacy

Small-group discussion supports both reading and writing by helping children clarify and extend their thoughts. It gives them something to write about and improves their understanding of what they read. The more sophisticated their own thinking in tasks such as explaining, planning or problem-solving, and especially in understanding feelings and emotion, the better they will be at understanding complex narratives, implicit meaning, and characterisation. A more sophisticated talker and thinker will be a more sophisticated reader.

Discussion work feeds more directly into both independent writing and comprehension work. Whenever children are set a writing exercise they should discuss it first in partner work or discussion groups. This allows them to share and develop ideas without being accused of copying or cheating – they think together but write separately – and also helps them to plan and organise what they are going to write, explain and clarify their ideas, and establish connections between one idea and another.

Most other literacy-support skills should be in place by this stage, but discussion work can also promote awareness, understanding and use of both reading and writing. Factual topics and questions will promote awareness and use of different types of information source. Discussing their independent reading with others will help children to reflect on what they read and why they read it. Discussing their writing, after they have done it, will help them reflect on what they wrote and why they wrote it in the way they did.

Child's name	Band 1	Will join in discussions with other children	Keeps to the topic	Will seek or give clarification	Band 2	Can discuss with others what they know or need to find out	Can discuss with others what they need to make or do something	Can explain why someone did something		Competent	Developing	Delayed
_____												
_____												
_____												
_____												
_____												
_____												
_____												
_____												
_____												
_____												
_____												
_____												
_____												
_____												
_____												
_____												
_____												
_____												
_____												
_____												

● Children who lack any of the behaviours in Band 1 are identified as *Delayed*, even if they have some of the behaviours in Band 2.

● Children who have all the behaviours in Band 1 but lack any of the behaviours in Band 2 are identified as *Developing*.

● Children who have all the behaviours in both Bands are identified as *Competent*.

Teaching Speaking and Listening © Ann Locke (Bloomsbury Publishing plc, 2013)

Child's name

Basic discussion skills

												Joins in discussion with other children
												Responds appropriately to others, e.g. questions or comments
												Will listen to others and not interrupt
												Keeps to the topic
												Doesn't monopolise, allows others their turn
												Makes relevant suggestions
												Comments on other people's suggestions
												Seeks clarification when needed
												Gives clarification when needed

Sharing knowledge

												Can contribute their own current knowledge
												Can discuss what is currently known in the group
												Can discuss what needs to be found out
												Can discuss how to find it out
												Can report findings back to the group
												Can comment on or ask questions about other children's findings
												Can report what the group has found out

Discussion Skills, Checklist 2

Planning and problem solving

One Step at a Time

Child's name

Explaining

												Can explain why or how something happened
												Can explain why someone did something
												Can describe an activity in sequence, step by step
												Can describe what a piece of equipment does
												Can describe what you do to make it work
												Can discuss why certain things happen or why we do them

Planning

												Can give an account of something they are about to make or do
												Can describe the tools and materials they need
												Can agree a plan with others
												Can list the steps in order
												Can discuss what will or should happen
												Can discuss what might or could happen
												Can discuss the success of a plan, and suggest improvements

Problem solving

												Can discuss what the problem is
												Can join with others in exploring possible solutions
												Can join with others in evaluating possible solutions
												Can discuss the success of an attempted solution and suggest improvements

CHAPTER 11 DISCUSSION SKILLS   **161**

Child's name

Negotiation

												Can outline or summarise the problem
												Can outline or summarise different interests or points of view
												Can explain or justify different points of view
												Can consider possible solutions
												Can state and justify their preferred solution

Understanding emotion

												Can identify and describe what the characters in a story might be feeling
												Can identify and describe what another child might be feeling in an imagined situation
												Can describe their own emotions
												Can discuss thoughts and feelings with other people, commenting, asking questions, etc.
												Can describe the situations in which various emotions occur
												Can describe their physical response to various emotions
												Can identify the impact of emotions on their behaviour
												Can identify the impact of their emotions on other people
												Can discuss ways of responding to or dealing with their feelings

Discussion Skills

Vocabulary wordlist

Discussion vocabulary

Verbs		Other words
agree	improve	atlas
argue	investigate	contents
ask	look for	correct
change your mind	negotiate	dictionary
check	notice	encyclopaedia
compare	plan	false
concentrate	predict	idea
contribute	prefer	impossible
co-operate	prepare	incorrect
decide	search	index
describe	settle (an argument)	information
disagree	solve (a problem)	possible
discover	suggest	problem
discuss	summarise	reasons
explain	think about	sure
find out	understand	topic
guess		uncertain

Feelings and emotion

Contrasting pairs		Other words	
afraid	brave	affectionate	jealous
bored	interested	angry	kind
confident	anxious	annoyed	lazy
excited	frightened	comfortable	nasty
happy	sad	cross	nice
foolish	sensible	curious	pleased
friendly	lonely	determined	scared
generous	selfish	disappointed	shy
glad	upset	enjoyable	silly
proud	ashamed	fair	sorry
surprised	calm	greedy	tense
		helpful	thoughtful
		hurt	violent
		irritated	worried

Teaching Speaking and Listening © Ann Locke (Bloomsbury Publishing plc, 2013)

NOTES ON CHECKLIST 1

Learning through discussion

This checklist sets out the basic skills that children need to hold a discussion, for learning and conveying information.

Basic discussion skills

This skill focuses on the mechanics of holding a discussion rather than the content. Almost any topic will do to practise these basic skills, but one place to start might be the topic of discussion itself, with questions like: Why is talking together a good idea? What can you learn from other children? Why do you need to wait your turn? Why do you need to listen carefully? What can you do if you don't understand something?

Extending knowledge

This skill is about discussion as a means to learning. Children need to be able to summarise their current knowledge and share and explore their ideas with other children. They need to be able to discuss what they need to know and how to find it out, then they need to be able to bring this knowledge back to the group and share it.

These skills will require at least two sessions for each topic. Children first need to discuss what they know already, what they need to find out, and how they can go about finding it. Then they need time to discover the information in whatever way suits them or the topic – with or without adult help; singly, in pairs, or as a group – before reporting back and discussing their findings.

Possible topics and questions include:

● finding out about wool, plastic, light, sound, etc.:
  Where does wool come from? What else do you know about wool? What questions have you got? What don't you know? How can you find out more? What new things did you learn? etc.

● finding out about pirates, Vikings, the World Cup:
  What do you know about pirates? What do the other children know? How many questions about pirates can you think of? Where will you find the answers? Who is going to find out? etc.

● finding out about your town, where people work, how your grandparents used to live, what we need to be healthy:
  How much do you know already? What else would you like to know? How can you find that out? Where can you find it? What did you learn? etc.

NOTES ON CHECKLIST 2

Planning and problem solving

This checklist is about learning how to give explanations and using discussion to plan and solve problems. In each case children may find it easier if they can talk about two or three examples first, in a general way, before being asked to work in detail on a particular case.

Explaining

If children are to learn they obviously need to be able to understand an explanation, but the ability to give an explanation, in terms that others can understand, is every bit as important. It requires attention to detail and sequencing skills, the ability to analyse a process into component parts and state them in order. It also requires awareness of other people's perspectives, of what can be taken for granted and what they need to know or be told. Barrier games, where children work in pairs with one child having to describe to the other something which the other child cannot see, are a good way of developing these skills, especially in children who find group discussion difficult.

The checklist covers several different kinds of explanation: why something happened, why someone did something, what something is, how it works, and why things happen as they do. In each case it is important to choose things that are already familiar to the children, so they can concentrate on how to explain it, rather than deciding what the explanation is.

Possible topics and questions include:

- how to get ready for school, plan a picnic, borrow a book from the library:
  What are all the things you need to do? Have you left anything out? Which one do you do first? What do you do next? What do you do last? etc.

- how to work a computer, a DVD player, a mobile phone:
  What do you need to do? What order do you need to do them in? Have you left anything out? etc.

- why something broke/how it got broken, why/how something melted or got burnt, how/why a pet died, someone got hurt:
  What happened? How did it happen? Could anyone/anything have stopped it? How? etc.

- why someone fell over, was late for school, went to London:
  Do you know why it happened? Would that have happened to you/would you have done it? What might have changed it? etc.

- why we live in houses, clean our teeth, go to school:
  Do you know why? What would happen if we didn't? How can you find out more? etc.

Planning

At this age children can be very impetuous; they tend to launch themselves into things without thinking. This part of the checklist helps them to think through an activity first, what they need to do and how they need to do it, and how to evaluate their planning.

Discussion topics for teaching these skills can be based around familiar routines and activities or selected from curriculum topics. Almost any project or experiment can be the basis of a planning exercise, though cooking is one activity where planning can make all the difference! Possible topics and questions include:

- making a model, birthday cards, biscuits, a scrapbook:
  What do you need to do? What things will you need to do it with? Will you need any help? What should you do first? What will you do next? What will you do after that? etc.

- getting ready for school, a birthday party, a class trip, a music lesson:
  What are the things you need to do? Can you list them in order? Have you left anything out? etc.

- preparing the classroom for routine activities, or for special events like a class concert, a party, a parents' evening:
  What do we need to do? What things do we need? What will happen if we forget something? etc.

- planning a project like a trip to a local country park to find out about flowers or insects:
  What will we look for? What do we want to find out? How can we find it out? How will we remember? When we get back to school, what will we do with what we have learnt?

- planning an experiment to compare weights, bouncing balls, ways of defrosting a bottle of milk:
  What things can you think of trying? What apparatus do you need? What should you do first? How can you compare/measure the results? What did you find out? etc.

The last two items introduce predictions (what will happen if…) and possibilities (what could or might happen). Possible topics and questions include:

- what will happen if it snows, the paint jars leak, the car runs out of petrol:
  Do you know what will happen? How can you find out what will happen? What can we do if that happens? What can we do now to get ready/stop it happening? etc.

- what would happen if the bell didn't go, the teachers forgot to come to school:
  What difference would it make? Would it matter? What would you do? What would happen next? etc.

- what could happen if you run across the road without looking, throw fireworks:
  What might happen? Does it matter? What would you do/say? How can we stop it happening? etc.

- what might happen if you go on holiday, go to a new school, get a new car:
  What would you like to happen? What wouldn't you like to happen? What else might happen? Which of them do you think will happen? Can you make them happen, or stop them happening? etc.

Problem solving

This section is about deciding how to do things. Conflicts, where people want to do different things, are dealt with in the next checklist under Negotiation. Like planning, problem solving requires children to think about something before they launch themselves into it. They have to consider the options and evaluate them before deciding on a course of action.

These skills will require at least two sessions for each topic. The children first need to discuss possible solutions. Then they to need to try one out, before discussing and evaluating the results. Almost any practical topic – in science, environmental studies, IT, etc. – can be set first as a problem to be discussed, then as an activity to be tried and evaluated. Other possible topics and questions include:

- how to clean up if someone spills sand, water, milk:
  What do we need to do? How can we do it? Which is the best way? How well will it work? How well did it work? etc.

- how to keep a drink warm, catch a kitten/dog/spider without hurting it (or getting hurt), get a cat down from a tree:
  What do you need to do? What ideas have you got? How well will they work? Which is the best idea? etc.

- how to mix paints to make orange or yellow, make a paper bridge for a toy car to drive over, keep warm in the playground when it's cold:
  How can you do that? What are all the different ideas you've got? Which is the best idea? How well will it work? How well did they work? Which was the best idea? etc.

- what to do if someone hurts themselves in the playground, loses their library book, needs to practise their reading:
  How can we help? What do we need to do? How can we do it? etc.

- how to stop children losing their gloves, wasting paper, running in the corridor:
  Why does it matter? Can we help? What can we do? Which idea is best? etc.

NOTES ON CHECKLIST 3

Negotiation and emotional literacy

Negotiation is working out a common course of action when people have different needs or wishes. It requires and develops an understanding of different points of view. At this level, especially with older children, the teacher can encourage children to identify situations which they themselves are finding difficult or problematic, to use as discussion topics, though there is the danger that as discussion becomes more personal it also becomes more heated. But discussion can also help children identify, describe and explain their feelings to themselves and to others. This is important for emotional literacy and the ability of children to manage their feelings, control their own behaviour, and respond appropriately to the behaviour of others.

Negotiation

Coming to an agreement or compromise about what to do in a situation where people have conflicting plans and interests is perhaps the most important skill we need to live and work together. It requires being able to understand other people's point of view, and being able to modify your own position to fit in with them. Negotiation is also important as a way of giving children practice in explaining and justifying themselves, or giving reasons for their own attitudes and opinions.

The teacher should first use a whole-class lesson to explain that we sometimes have situations where people disagree because they all want different things, so they have to talk about them and decide what to do. She can give some familiar examples, such as sharing toys, making too much mess or noise, or deciding who should clear things away, and talk them over one at a time: she can, for example, explain why we need to share, what happens if we don't, and what we can do if someone doesn't want to share.

Once children are familiar with these ideas, the teacher can explain that people sometimes have different ideas about what is the right or best thing to do, and we have to consider their views as well as our own. This isn't a matter of being right or wrong but of finding a solution, possibly a compromise, that everyone can agree on. She should also discuss the consequences of not being able to come to an agreement, and the problems this can lead to among children, adults, and nations.

When disputes arise in the normal course of events, as they surely will, the teacher should discuss them then and there, if appropriate, and praise any positive responses or attempts to negotiate, without unnecessarily criticising any negative or selfish behaviour. She can then go back to these situations in a whole-class lesson, when all children are present, but concentrating on how the problem could have been resolved, rather than how it arose in the first place.

Possible topics and questions include:

● what to do if children want to play different games, watch different things on TV, play with the toys someone else is playing with:
Why is this a problem? What do you think should happen? What should we do if some people have a different idea about what to do? What should we do if we all agree about what to do, and then someone doesn't do it? etc.

● how to decide who should do an enjoyable or boring job in the classroom, like taking a message to another teacher, putting the reading books out, or tidying up after a messy lesson:
Does it matter? Why? What would you want to happen? Would that be fair to everyone? etc.

● what to do if someone won't play with other children, breaks another child's toy, is being naughty, finds something someone lost, and won't give it back:
Why is this a problem? What might happen? What can you do about it? What do you think should happen? Is that being nice to everyone? etc.

Understanding emotions

The checklist lists a number of ways in which children might talk about their feelings and emotions: what they feel, when they feel it, how it affects their behaviour, how it affects other people, and so on. They may find this easier if they start by discussing the feelings of characters in stories, or what they or their friends might feel in various imagined situations, rather than actual feelings in real situations. Familiar stories or imaginary situations can be topics for the first few discussion sessions:

Why did he do that? What do you think he was feeling? What else would he feel like doing? How did the other people feel? How would you feel if...? What would you want to do? What would be the best/right thing to do? What would your friends do?

Children need to develop this understanding of many different types of emotion, from basic feelings like pleasure, fear and anger through to more subtle emotions like confidence, boredom and jealousy. Some of these may be unfamiliar, in the sense that they haven't thought about them before, and may need to be explained carefully with familiar examples. How far the teacher goes into more complex or more subtle emotions will depend on how well the children are dealing with them in their discussion groups.

The teacher should start by selecting a few simple emotions in contrasting pairs like *happy/sad*. There are several other examples in the Vocabulary wordlist. She can introduce each pair in a whole-class lesson, explaining them both and the difference between them, and giving examples. She will probably want to accentuate the positive emotion, but children may identify more quickly with the negative emotion. The single emotions in the wordlist tend to be more subtle and can be introduced later.

The teacher should work through several different emotions in turn, setting the discussion groups simple questions like:

What makes you happy? What makes you sad? When are you happy? When are you sad? Why? How does it feel?

before going back to the beginning to set more demanding questions like:

What do you do when you're feeling angry? What can you do about it? How does that make other people feel? What can they do about it?

How far and how fast she goes will depend on how well children respond to these questions in their discussion groups. Items on the checklist should be credited only when children can demonstrate the skills with several different emotions.

Chapter 12 Vocabulary work

Vocabulary is clearly essential for language. Words are what give language its content; without them we would have no language at all. Vocabulary also seems to be the motor for grammatical development. The more words that children know, and the more different types of word they know, the more readily they develop grammatical forms. It is easy to think that 'vocabulary' means nouns, verbs and adjectives but children also need to learn adverbs, prepositions and connectives like *if*, *because* and *although*, both to understand the sentences they hear and read and to add variety and structure to their own sentences. Children with a limited vocabulary will have a limited sentence structure as well.

Vocabulary is crucial for children's learning. The more words they understand, the more they can learn from what others say, and from what they read; and the more words they are able to use for themselves, the more they will be able to learn and find out, for example by answering and asking questions. If they don't have the vocabulary they won't know how to answer or what to ask.

Vocabulary is equally crucial for teaching. It's not just that we have to use words for teaching. We also use them to bring the outside world into the classroom. Early learning is based on physical activity with physical objects – touching things, playing with them, exploring them – and even when children enter school, handling things is still the best way of learning about them. But we cannot bring everything into the classroom, so we teach children about the world through language that reports and describes the world outside. The more words that children know and the better they understand them, the more easily we can extend their learning.

Vocabulary also helps to develop children's thinking. The words we know shapes what we can think, and even what we observe in the world around us. When the Inuit learn several different words for different kinds of snow they are, at the same time, learning to notice the different kinds of snow that those words name. As children progress through school the words they need to know become more detailed and more subtle (*implausible*, *contradictory*, *deceptive*; *approximately*, *simultaneously*, *freely*), increasing their capacity to reflect, speculate and evaluate. Words convey ideas, and the more varied and precise our vocabulary, the more varied and precise our thoughts can be.

Vocabulary contributes to literacy by enabling children to understand what they read, both directly, because they know what the words mean, and indirectly, because the larger their vocabulary, the better they will be at grasping the meaning of a passage as a whole, and therefore at guessing the meaning of words they do not know, and then adding them to their vocabulary. Vocabulary also gives children the resources for independent writing. The wider their vocabulary, the more accurate, detailed and complex their writing can be.

The link between vocabulary and literacy is obvious enough. The link between vocabulary and other curriculum subjects may be less so. Children need the relevant vocabulary to understand new subjects and topics, and the wider their vocabulary the deeper that understanding will be. Here too they need to know not just the crucial nouns, verbs and adjectives but also the adverbs, prepositions and connectives that provide detail, structure and insight. 'Articulate vocabulary is not simply a gloss to improve the appearance of students' work', writes a secondary school history teacher (Woodcock, 2005), 'but a fundamental tool with which to develop conceptual understanding':

> Words are tools, not just for speaking and writing but also for thought and developing new ideas... In order to develop students' understanding of the Second World War, I experimented with providing them with new vocabulary, which they would not otherwise have known or chosen to use... By encouraging them to consider the deep, varied meanings and implications of words, I hoped to introduce new ideas, new ways of thinking about events, and new means of expressing subtle, precise ideas.

Vocabulary is also an important element in what is sometimes called emotional literacy or emotional intelligence. This involves a number of things, including understanding your own feelings and expressing them appropriately, and being able to recognise and respond to other people's feelings and behaviour. To do this appropriately, children need to have the vocabulary to identify and discuss a variety of different feelings and emotions, their own and other's, both positive and negative.

Vocabulary is, however, easy to take for granted, and teachers sometimes unwittingly use language that is too complex or too sophisticated for some of the children they are talking to. Vocabulary that seems obvious to adults may not always be familiar to children. A young child who understands *in* may still be confused at being asked to *join in* something or *stand in line*. Older children, similarly, may seem slow to learn only because they don't fully understand the words being used to teach a new topic or subject.

Moreover, if teachers teach vocabulary explicitly, this will not only ensure that all children know the words they need for classroom learning but also make them more aware of the role that vocabulary plays in their learning. It will help them to appreciate the importance of finding out – and encourage them to ask – the meanings of any words or expressions they don't understand, not only in their reading but in their classroom lessons.

Despite all this, vocabulary work is treated as an optional element in *One Step at a Time*, except for Getting Started and Discussion Skills. This is partly because *One Step* focuses on other language skills that are equally important but less likely to be familiar to teachers and therefore more easily neglected. Staff, like the children they teach, can only be expected to handle so much at a time, and developing children's use of language is also a way of developing vocabulary, as well as sentence structure and fluency.

It is also because some vocabulary teaching is going to happen anyway. Vocabulary work is part and parcel of normal curriculum teaching, especially when teaching reading and spelling ('Do you know what that word means'?) or when introducing new subjects or topics. Teaching any new topic is, in large part, teaching new vocabulary.

But there are many important words – especially adjectives, prepositions and adverbs – that do not belong to any particular curriculum area and are easily neglected. They are also words that many children are likely to find difficult because they are more abstract than the concrete nouns and verbs of early vocabulary, or because they are used in different ways in different contexts. As usual, most children will pick up most of these words from normal classroom interaction, but some may need to be taught them explicitly and systematically. This chapter describes how staff can do this.

Teaching vocabulary

Vocabulary is vast, typically running into thousand of words even at the pre-school stage. By the time children leave school it will be tens of thousands. It is hopelessly unrealistic to expect staff to assess or teach all the words that children need to know for progress in school. At the very least, they need to be selective.

Vocabulary wordlists

The model for teaching spoken language in Chapter 2 identified four key types of vocabulary:

● early vocabulary

● the vocabulary of properties and relations

● the vocabulary of feelings and emotion

● topic vocabulary.

Topic vocabulary will vary with the curriculum but each level of *One Step at a Time* provides a list of 100 essential words chosen from the first three categories. For Getting Started they are the early vocabulary that children seem most likely to learn first. For Conversation Skills, Listening Skills and Narrative Skills they are a combination of the vocabulary of properties and relations and the vocabulary of feelings and emotion. For Discussion Skills they are the vocabulary of feelings and emotion, supplemented by the vocabulary of discussion, agreement and negotiation that children will need to be using in their discussion groups. Each list is intended to be supplemented with topic vocabulary from the current curriculum.

Most children should know most of these words already, but some may not and the only way of knowing for sure which is which is by checking each word and each child individually. But checking even 100 words with all children would be very demanding in time and resources, so *One Step at a Time* suggests instead a phased approach to vocabulary work. Except for Getting Started and Discussion Skills, where vocabulary is an essential part of the programme, staff should concentrate on skills teaching first, and not introduce specific vocabulary work until everyone – children and staff – is fully comfortable with that.

The teacher can first select three or four words from the relevant Vocabulary wordlist. It is often convenient to teach several words from the same category (quality, colour, etc.) at the same time, but contrasting pairs like *big* and *small* or *quick* and *slow*, or words with similar sounds or meanings like *big* and *biggest* or *loud* and *noisy*, should be avoided with younger children because they are likely to find them confusing.

She can then identify another four to six items of essential topic vocabulary from current curriculum teaching. In the early years these 'topics' are likely to be the seasons, festivities, trips or outings and other current activities, but with older children they will be curriculum subjects, including maths (words like *rectangle*, *multiply*, *graph*, etc.) and literacy (*sentence*, *verb*, *comma*, *author*, etc.). Before introducing any new topic the teacher should first identify the key words that the children in her class are going to need to know, the words that name and describe the things they will be learning. She can even include her class in this process, going over her list with them to see which ones they know already, and adding any words that seem difficult or unfamiliar. Talking about the words will be talking about the topic, and vice versa, and discussing the words that need to be learnt will help children reflect on their vocabulary and understand how words are important and why they need to know them.

In this way the teacher will arrive at a list of six to ten words for current teaching. This list can be varied week by week, phasing some words out and some new ones in, but some words may need to be featured over several weeks. It is also a good idea to return from time to time to any words that some children have found particularly difficult. When the class has worked through all the words in the Vocabulary wordlist, more comprehensive vocabulary lists can easily be obtained from the internet.

Classroom intervention

The teacher can now feature the selected words as her 'words of the week' or 'this week's special words'. She should start by introducing and explaining them at the beginning of each week and displaying them prominently in the classroom for reference by everyone. These words can then be included and featured on every possible occasion over the rest of the week, in whole-class lessons, group work and one-to-one interaction. Children who are reading can be encouraged to consult the list for themselves, looking out for those words in lessons and independent reading, and using them in their own talk and writing. Topic vocabulary will be taught more explicitly as part of topic teaching, but the vocabularies of properties and relations and of feelings and emotions also need to be taught more systematically. That is precisely why they are featured on the wordlists.

Early vocabulary learning requires frequent opportunities first to hear a word used in context and then to use it for yourself. This typically involves four steps:

● experience of the object, activity or characteristic that gives the word its meaning.
  Children will have to get used to unfamiliar things first, before they can grasp the meaning

- understanding that word when used by others
- being able to use the word if prompted or encouraged (for example, being asked to name something, or being given a sentence to complete: 'What's this?', 'It's your … [sock]')
- using the word spontaneously.

Older or more able children may do these things very quickly, almost simultaneously. Others may learn much more slowly. Especially with more abstract terms there can be quite a long time between children understanding the words and starting to use them for themselves.

Younger children will always find it easier to learn new vocabulary through being involved in familiar physical activities where they can handle real objects, rather than looking at books or pictures. Doing or making things (cutting out a *square*, celebrating a *birthday*, holding a *clock*, colouring something *red*), or playing with things that are *big*, *soft* or *heavy* will help them understand and remember nouns and adjectives. Once they are beginning to use a word staff can introduce less familiar contexts, and pictures as well as real objects, to generalise and consolidate their learning. Staff will find it useful to build up a stock of suitable toys and objects for teaching specific words, and pictures and stories for consolidation, and for teaching feelings and emotion vocabulary and words like *night-time* and *birthday*.

Physical activity seems particularly important for the vocabulary of properties and relations. The best way to learn words of position and movement, for example, is by putting things – or even better, putting themselves – *in*, *on* or *under* something, or moving them – or themselves – *through* something or *away* from it, or *slowly* or *backwards*. PE and games, and tidying up after an activity, provide good opportunities for teaching these words. Words of quantity, similarly, can be learnt by picking up a lot of toys, finding *another* one, or putting them *all* in a box until it is *nearly* full.

The obvious way to teach some adjectives and adverbs is in contrasting pairs: *noisy* and *quiet*, for example, or *quickly* and *slowly*. But young children can find this confusing. *Noisy* should instead be contrasted with *not noisy*. *Quiet* should not be introduced until some time later, and should be contrasted with *not quiet*, not with *noisy*. Opposites should only be introduced when both words have been established separately.

Older children can be taught vocabulary in curriculum lessons and classroom activities like talk-time, circle-time and story-time, and using pictures and stories rather than real objects and toys. But some words – particularly more abstract ones – are still best taught through activity or movement: measuring the *length* of something, facing in a different *direction*, or talking *softly*. There are some abstract words, however, like *number*, *soon*, *tomorrow* or *clockwise*, that need to be taught through explanation and discussion: 'Who knows what a *number* is?', 'What does it mean if we're going to do something *soon*?, 'Which way does a clock go?'.

This applies also to the vocabulary of feelings and emotion. Stories and classroom or playground incidents may provide opportunities for highlighting and teaching these words: 'Why was that fox *clever*?', 'Why did Jenny feel so *sad*?', 'You all surprised me', 'That was *exciting*, wasn't it?'. But they may sometimes need to be explained more formally: 'Who knows what *thirsty* means?', 'What happens if someone is *angry*?', 'What makes us all *happy*?', 'How can we be *friendly* to each other?'. The teacher can then build on the children's answers to explain and develop the concept at a level they can understand, or use stories or anecdotes to develop their understanding. To help them understand these words fully it is useful to highlight all three aspects of the emotion: the contexts in which it typically occurs ('What would make you afraid?', 'What if you saw a tiger?'), the typical response ('What do you think you would do?') and the internal feeling ('How would it make you feel inside?').

Monitoring progress

All this should ensure that all children are taught the vocabulary from the wordlist. But it will not ensure that all children actually do know – that is, can both use and understand – all these words, bearing in mind that it is always easy for some children to escape detailed notice in a busy classroom, and that some of those who appear to understand may simply be copying other children. The only practical way to monitor individual learning systematically is through small-group intervention using vocabulary checklists on the model of small-group skills work. This is unlikely to be necessary – or even possible – with all children in the class. But vocabulary teaching at a whole-class level may identify some children as having particular difficulty in acquiring new language, and it may sometimes be possible – or even necessary – to provide these children with dedicated small-group vocabulary work, supported as usual by informal interaction with individual children.

Much of the advice for small-group vocabulary work will be the same as for small-group skills work, which by this stage both children and staff should be thoroughly familiar with. In particular, the simplest way to focus and guide intervention and monitor individual progress is to enter all the words of the week on to a vocabulary checklist, and continue working on each item until all children in the group have learnt it.

There are, however, two aspects to 'knowing' a word or phrase: understanding it when used by others (comprehension) and being able to use it correctly yourself (expression). Understanding usually comes before use. Parents are often astonished at how much their toddlers understand, long before they start speaking. It's the same when adults are learning another language: they can understand what other people are saying to them even if they are not sure how to say it themselves.

Children need to be able to do both, and either on its own is unreliable. Children may seem to understand what others say, when they are simply copying other children or imitating the teacher. Some children use lots of words without really understanding what they are saying. The best way to assess, teach and monitor vocabulary learning, always, is through one-to-one conversation. In conversation, staff can introduce the word, observe the response, encourage the child to use it for himself, and check that he is using it appropriately. This is why systematic vocabulary work ideally needs to be in small groups, supported by informal interaction.

Appendix 1

Some specific issues

One Step at a Time is intended to provide differentiated teaching for all children in mainstream education. There will, however, be some children who have a specific difficulty with spoken language, or perhaps with spoken English. This appendix offers some guidance on the five most common groups.

Children who don't talk much

Getting Started is intended for children aged three to four or five who are still learning basic language and need to be helped to develop a wider vocabulary and simple two or three-word utterances. Older children who are still at this stage, or don't talk at all, are likely to need specialist support. But there may be some older children who do have basic language but still say very little or seem reluctant to use what language they do have.

The 'Tips for encouraging talk in young children' in Chapter 7 are always relevant but obviously need to be adapted for older children. What you talk about will be different and you will both be using more advanced language, but the best approach is still to share interest in activities and use conversation to extend and expand meaning and model more complex sentence structures. Computer work and 'hands-on' subjects like art and design or science and technology provide some of the best opportunities for developing interactive conversation with older children. You should also allow plenty of time for them to formulate their response. Children vary considerably in the speed with which they process language, and some of them will need much more time than we might expect to make sense of what we say or find a response.

However, self-confidence is often the most important factor. Children with limited spoken language can easily feel foolish – or be made to feel foolish – if they are awkward or hesitant when faced with a task that others take for granted, like talking, and may seize up completely if any pressure is put on them. If they can be made to feel secure and supported they can usually be helped to speak more easily.

There are a number of things that staff can do to promote children's confidence and self-esteem, and support their social interaction as well as their language skills:

- Highlight success: Make positive comments and appreciate effort wherever possible. Use small rewards like a smiley badge, or a visit to or from the headteacher.
- Promote friendships: Group each child with one or two sympathetic, more confident

children to encourage friendships. Choose children with similar interests who are likely to be friendly without being dominating or over-protective.

- Give responsibility: Find simple classroom tasks for them to perform alone or with a friend, like handing out papers or pencils or taking messages to other classrooms or the school office. These can work up from written messages that don't need a reply to verbal messages to fetch an object or bring back a written reply, and eventually to verbal messages needing a verbal reply.

- Shared work: Get them to work with more confident children, e.g. paired reading, or help with younger children in a lower class, e.g. reading a story or playing a small-group game, but without singling them out, i.e. using other children too.

Children with unclear speech

Unclear speech is a common problem in the early years. Most three-year-olds are still establishing the full range of speech sounds, so delay in establishing some sounds and other minor difficulties like a tendency to stammer, hesitate or repeat sounds or words, especially when excited, is not usually a cause for concern. The important thing is not to make an issue of their speech by correcting them, making them repeat themselves, or otherwise embarrassing them. Staff should instead provide good, clear models of correct speech, speaking slowly and carefully themselves, and do everything they can to support and encourage these children and build up their self-esteem if they seem shy or nervous.

If children do not respond to this fairly quickly a possible cause of continuing unclear speech is an undiagnosed hearing problem. Ear infections ('glue ear') are very common at this age and can have a serious effect on children's learning and social interaction as well as their speaking and listening. Staff should keep an eye out for tell-tale signs like a failure to understand or concentrate, especially in noisy situations, and try a simple test like choosing a quiet time to talk softly behind a child's back and see if he notices. Any child with a suspected hearing difficulty should be referred for a full hearing assessment and sat at the front of the room in a place where they can see the teacher clearly, and any other children who may be speaking. These children will also be helped by the listening activities described in Chapter 9. For further advice see the Procedures Handbook in *Teaching Talking* (Locke and Beech, 2005), Chapters 2 and 6.

If there is no problem with hearing, continuing unclear speech, especially in older children, may be a sign of an underlying language or comprehension difficulty.

Children with unclear language

Whether or not their speech is unclear, some children may be difficult or even impossible to understand because their language itself is confused or jumbled, seeming to make little sense. With young children this may be a temporary phase or the result of a hearing problem, but if it persists it can indicate a specific difficulty with language or comprehension. These children need expert support, and should be referred to a speech and language therapist as soon as possible. Here too, staff should not try to correct or improve their speech, but they may be almost incomprehensible and there does need to be some means of communication. Nothing is more stressful, for teacher and child, than not being able to understand each other. However, they will usually become more comprehensible with familiarity, and the easiest way to 'tune-in' to their speech is by getting them to talk, and listening carefully to what they say, in shared contexts where the meaning should be obvious to you both. Moreover, other children are often better at understanding and communicating with them, and may be able to interpret for you both.

Children for whom English is an additional language

Children may be classified as Delayed on the initial screens for all sorts of reasons. For some it will be because English is not their home language. *One Step at a Time* will be equally effective with these children. Getting Started, in particular, can be very useful in developing both language and confidence in children whose knowledge of English is very limited or who find school a strange and frightening experience. Older children with very limited English will also benefit from working through the Starter Vocabulary which is part of the Getting Started programme.

Most of these children will improve rapidly and, once started, should progress through the programme more quickly than delayed English-speaking children. But some may also be delayed in their home language. For this reason it will be very helpful if the programme can be operated in their home language as well as in English, either by using home-language speakers in the classroom or by involving parents. This will indicate whether the apparent delay is just in English or in spoken language more generally. There may be concern that working in two languages at the same time will be confusing for these children, but the evidence is that while children who are learning more than one language may be slightly slower than other children in establishing either language, in the longer term their spoken language actually benefits overall.

Children with special educational needs

A special educational need can affect spoken language either directly, because it is or includes a difficulty specifically with language or communication (such as specific language impairment or autistic spectrum difficulties), or indirectly, because it affects the acquisition of spoken language (such as visual or auditory impairments). *One Step at a Time* should be very effective with the latter group but children who have difficulties specifically with language or communication are likely to progress more slowly than other children in the class.

Children with significant difficulties will benefit from the Getting Started level of the programme but may be slow to develop more advanced skills. Schools will have their own policies and procedures for supporting these children, tailored to the particular needs of the individual child. They should be included in whole-class and small-group language work as far as is possible and practicable without putting them under unnecessary pressure or delaying other children in the class. But they can also be given individual support by using a personalised programme like *Teaching Talking* (Locke and Beech, 2005).

Teaching Talking operates at three levels: identification and initial support using initial screens and classroom strategies; small-group intervention using language records and small-group language work; and detailed profiling using detailed profiles and individual intervention. These correspond to the pre-SEN, Action and Action Plus levels in the revised *Special Educational Needs Code of Practice for England and Wales* (DfES, 2001) and can be used to plan intervention in accordance with the code of practice.

Children who are doing *One Step at a Time* will already be doing small-group language work but the *Teaching Talking* language records will help to provide an individual education plan. The detailed profiles will be particularly useful for children needing individual intervention because they assess several areas of development, not just spoken language. The Procedures Handbook, Activities Handbook, and the detailed profiles can all be purchased separately.

Appendix 2

The development of language and communication from birth to nine years

A summary of typical childhood development as a guide to progress or delay in the early years.

From birth to one year most babies learn to:

- recognise familiar people as a source of comfort, pleasure and interest and are motivated to communicate with them
- use their senses to explore and manipulate objects, starting the process of making sense of the world and identifying things they will soon want to communicate about
- look at simple pictures, for several seconds
- attract and hold other people's attention through body movement, gesture and vocalisation
- co-operate and take turns in their interaction with other people
- 'tune-in' to the speech patterns of the people around them and understand single words or simple phrases used in familiar situations
- initiate contact with familiar adults and other children.

Between one and two years most children learn to:

- understand and respond to simple questions and instructions
- produce single words and use them to indicate things of interest, identify needs, gain attention or share an interest with others
- copy new words, and produce some speech sounds clearly
- enjoy simple speech-action games like 'Round and round the garden', and join in the actions
- identify familiar objects and actions in pictures, and look through picture books.

Between two and three years most children learn to:

- understand and produce a steadily increasing number of new words (by the age of three most children are able to use several hundred words confidently)
- link words together and show some awareness of grammatical features by, for example, using pronouns (*I, you, she, they*, etc.) or verb tenses (*was talking, jumped*, etc.)

- have regular conversations with familiar adults and children
- use language in different contexts, such as play, everyday routines (dressing, washing, eating, etc.) or talking about stories
- produce a good range of speech sounds accurately
- enjoy listening to and repeating simple rhymes
- discuss scenes in pictures and follow simple stories.

Between three and four years most children learn to:

- speak clearly and hold intelligible conversations with familiar and less familiar adults
- understand and use a vocabulary of several hundred to 2,000 or 3,000 words
- co-operate and converse with other children in a variety of play situations
- understand and use adult sentences and grammatical features
- use language for an increasing range of purposes, such as directing, asking questions, commenting, and expressing feelings
- repeat songs or rhymes from memory, and 'play' with words or sounds
- contribute to talking about past events and discussing the future
- use pencils, crayons, etc. to 'draw' on paper.

Between four and five years most children learn to:

- use conversation to co-ordinate behaviour with adults and/or children
- contribute actively to imaginative play, for example, by directing self and others through conversation, and taking different roles in group play
- use constructions like *why/because* and *if ... then* as a means of reasoning
- talk about present, past and future events, and can make a good attempt to retell a story, describe a recent event or talk about what they are going to do
- listen with interest to stories and relate them to their own experience
- 'read' books to themselves, possibly recognising some familiar words in print, such as their name
- enjoy games with speech sounds, such as clapping out the rhythm of words or phrases, recognising words that rhyme, or playing 'I spy'.
- use pencils, crayons, etc., to draw pictures and to 'write'
- read single words, at first in familiar, then in less familiar, contexts.

Between five and six years most children learn to:

- use language for an increasing number of educational purposes, such as observing people or animals, comparing objects, explaining, etc.
- recount recent experiences in chronological order, and predict possible future events

- appreciate that words can be written down, and show interest in having their own words written down, or attempt to write them themselves
- discriminate sounds in words and recognise that these can be written down as letters
- write some simple words accurately from memory
- write simple sentences (e.g. greetings, messages, answers to questions).

Between six and seven years most children learn to:

- work with other children to organise tasks and solve problems
- follow a lengthy sequence of ideas in stories, make predictions about possible developments to a story, and give reasons
- use language to negotiate and reach agreement with others
- read simple stories, and answer questions about what they have read
- use their reading to acquire new vocabulary
- tell a simple story or outline a sequence of events, prior to producing a written account
- write an increasing number of words from memory and produce simple sequences of ideas in writing
- use sound-letter links to read and spell unknown words
- produce short pieces of independent writing, using complete sentences.

Between seven and nine years most children learn to:

- plan and produce collaborative work in discussion with other children: for example, a short story, a simple play, an account of personal experience, or a scientific or mathematical investigation
- work with other children to identify problems and explore possible solutions
- follow extended directions or instructions and long stories or factual accounts
- discuss their own and other people's feelings and behaviour
- discuss possible improvements to their own or group work, such as the use of more effective vocabulary or corrections to illogical or incorrect sequences of ideas
- read independently for lengthy periods and use their reading to gain knowledge or find out answers to questions
- write for different purposes, both imaginative and factual
- know most of the rules of spelling, and use simple punctuation consistently.

References

Assessment Reform Group (2002), Assessment for Learning: 10 Principles: research–based principles to guide classroom practice. Available to download from: www.aaia.org.uk/afl/assessment-reform-group/

Boyer, E. L. (1991), *Ready to Learn*. Princeton, NJ: Carnegie Foundation for the Advancement of Teaching.

Crystal, D. (1989), *Listen to Your Child*. London: Penguin Books.

DfES (2001), *Special Educational Needs Code of Practice*. London: Department for Education and Skills.

DfES (2004), *Five Year Strategy for Children and Learners*. London: Department for Education and Skills.

DFE (2010), *The Importance of Teaching*. London: Department for Education.

Field, F., Today programme, BBC, 23 July 2011 (reported at www.bbc.co.uk/news/education-14324745).

Gross, J (2011), *Two Years On: final report of the Communication Champion for Children*. London: Office of the Communication Champion. Available to download from www.communicationmatters.org.uk/sites/default/files/downloads/news/2011_final_report_of_communication_champion.pdf)

Hart, B. and Risley, T. R. (1995), *Meaningful Differences in the Everyday Experience of Young American Children*. Baltimore, MD: Brookes Publishing.

Latham, D. (2002), *How Children Learn to Write: supporting and developing children's writing in schools*. London: Paul Chapman.

Law, J., Parkinson, A. and Tamnhe, R. (eds.) (1999), *Communication Difficulties in Childhood: a practical guide*. Abingdon: Radcliffe Publishing Ltd.

Locke, A (1985), *Living Language*. London: nferNelson.

Locke, A. (2006), *One Step at a Time*. London: Network Continuum Education.

Locke, A. and Beech, M. (2005), *Teaching Talking* (second edn). London: nferNelson.

Locke, A. and Ginsborg, J. (2003), 'Spoken Language in the Early Years: the cognitive and linguistic development of three- to five-year-old children from socio-economically deprived backgrounds'. *Education and Child Psychology*, 20(4), 68–79.

Locke, A., Ginsborg, J. and Peers, I. (2002), 'Development and Disadvantage: implications for the early years and beyond'. *International Journal of Language and Communication Disorders*, 37(1), 3–15.

Nippold, M. A. (1998), *Later Language Development: the school-age and adolescent years* (second edn). Austin, TX: PRO-ED

Ofsted (2005), *English 2000–05: a review of the inspection evidence* London: Ofsted.

Ofsted (2010), *Reading by Six: how the best schools do it*. London: Ofsted.

Ofsted (2012), 'Ofsted Chief Inspector calls for rapid improvement in literacy' (press release, 15 March 2012). London: Ofsted.

Pinker, S. (1994), *The Language Instinct*. London: Penguin Books.

Sage, R. (2005), 'Communicating with Students who have Learning and Behaviour Difficulties: a continuing professional development programme'. *Emotional and Behavioural Difficulties*, 10 (4), 281–297.

Roulstone, S, Law, J., Rush, R., Clegg, J. and Peters, T. (2011), *Investigating the Role of Language in Children's Early Educational Outcomes*. London: Department for Education.

Timperley, H., Wilson, A., Barrar, H. and Fung, I. (2007), *Teacher Professional Learning and Development*. Wellington, NZ: Ministry of Education.

Webster, A. (1987), 'Enabling language acquisition: the developmental evidence', *British Psychological Society*, Division of Educational and Child Psychology Newsletter, 27, 27–31.

Woodcock, J (2005), 'Latent meaning', *Times Educational Supplement*, 18 November 2005.

Index

thinking skills 14, 16, 17, 18, 34, 119, 146
time 117, 120
    understanding 118
toddlers 20
topic teaching 14
training 42–3
turn-taking 65, 87–8

unclear language 178–9
unclear speech 178
    older children 178
under-achievement 4, 6, 31
understanding 81, 92, 93, 96, 113, 117, 135,
        169, 174, 175
    assessment 113
USA
    Head Start 5

verb forms 15
verbal contact 49
verbs 13, 51, 54, 69, 171
    irregular 141
    modal 15
    tenses 118, 119, 120, 141, 143–5
video 73, 98, 125

visual impairments 179
visual-motor skills 81, 107, 135
vocabulary 2, 10, 12–13, 14, 17, 26, 28, 35, 36,
        39, 48, 52, 54, 55, 57, 59, 67, 76, 80, 101,
        118, 128, 154, 170–75
    checklists 175
    early years 13
    emotion 13, 101, 174
    feelings 13, 101, 174
    group work 175
    starter 51–2, 179
    teaching 172–5
    topic vocabulary 14, 35, 39, 172, 173
    wordlists 172–3
voice 126, 148

whole-class activities 99
whole-class work 74, 99, 124
word memory 116
word patterns 115
word sounds 116
word-finding 7
wordlists 154, 172
writing 39, 80, 106, 116, 118, 119, 133, 135, 158
    independent 133, 171